EARLY CHURCH FATHERS
SERIES EDITOR MICHAEL A. G. HAYKIN

CYPRIAN
OF HIS LIFE & IMPACT
CARTH-
AGE

BRIAN ARNOLD

CHRISTIAN
FOCUS

Unless otherwise indicated, Scripture quotations are from *The Holy Bible, English Standard Version*, copyright © 2001 by Crossway Bibles, a division of Good News Publishers. Used by permission. All rights reserved. ESV Text Edition: 2007.

Scripture quotations marked NASB are taken from *The New American Standard Bible®*, copyright © 1960, 1962, 1963, 1968, 1971, 1972, 1973, 1975, 1977, 1995 by The Lockman Foundation. Used by Permission. (www.Lockman.org)

Brian J. Arnold (PhD, The Southern Baptist Theological Seminary) teaches Systematic Theology and Church History at Phoenix Seminary in Phoenix, Arizona, U.S.A. Before this, Brian pastored for several years in western Kentucky. He is also the author of *Justification in the Second Century* (de Gruyter) and a forthcoming commentary on the *Epistle to Diognetus* with Michael A. G. Haykin.

Copyright © Brian J. Arnold 2017

Brian J. Arnold has asserted his right under the Copyright, Designs and Patents Act, 1988, to be identified as Author of this work.

paperback ISBN 978-1-5271-0099-2
epub ISBN 978-1-5271-0131-9
mobi ISBN 978-1-5271-0132-6

First published in 2017
by
Christian Focus Publications Ltd,
Geanies House, Fearn, Ross-shire.
IV20 1TW, Scotland.
www.christianfocus.com

A CIP catalogue record for this book is available from the British Library.

Cover designer: MOOSE77

Printed by Bell and Bain, Glasgow.

All rights reserved. No part of this publication may be reproduced, stored in a retrieval system, or transmitted, in any form, by any means, electronic, mechanical, photocopying, recording or otherwise without the prior permission of the publisher or a licence permitting restricted copying. In the U.K. such licences are issued by the Copyright Licensing Agency, Saffron House, 6-10 Kirby Street, London, EC1 8TS www.cla.co.uk.

There is a growing excitement about this series of volumes recounting the immense importance of the early Church Fathers in our circles and it is hugely encouraging to see this account of the significant life of Cyprian of Carthage by Brian J. Arnold. Immensely rewarding and full of exquisite detail, this book is a winner in every respect. More, please.

Derek W. H. Thomas
Senior Minister, First Presbyterian Church, Columbia, South Carolina,
Chancellor's Professor, Reformed Theological Seminary;
Teaching Fellow, Ligonier Ministries

Arnold, as an American evangelical, reaches across time and space to introduce a third-century North African theologian. He purposes neither to re-make Cyprian in his own image nor to discard the Carthaginian bishop on the ash heap of history. Resisting both temptations, Arnold rather insists that Cyprian can serve as a stimulating conversation partner within the contemporary context.

Paul Hartog
Adjunct Faculty, Biblical Studies,
Faith Baptist Bible College and Theological Seminary,
Ankeny, Iowa

Brian J. Arnold guides us to a compelling voice from the past at a time when we desperately need wisdom for the present. On every accessibly written and skilfully researched page, the life and legacy of Cyprian speaks with wisdom and captivating intensity. This is a valuable book for those seeking an informative and formative conversation with the church fathers. We would do well to listen.

Megan DeVore
Associate Professor of Church History and Early Christian Studies,
Colorado Christian University,
Lakewood, Colorado

A thought provoking, fascinating, stimulating and easy to read book on a theologian who loved church. It is a book about a great man that should change, challenge and bring joy every time you meet with and think about your church.

Steve Levy
Pastor, Mount Pleasant Baptist Church,
Swansea, Wales

CONTENTS

Series preface..9
A chronology of Cyprian's life...13
Preface 15

1. Cyprian of Carthage 23

2. Cyprian and his Controversies 63

3. Cyprian and the Church 91

4. Cyprian and the Christian Life 117

5. Cyprian and Contempory Christianity 147

Further Reading..153

DEDICATION

To Jameson and Natalie
Sources of joy and laughter

SERIES PREFACE

On reading the Church Fathers

By common definition, the Church Fathers are those early Christian authors who wrote between the close of the first century, right after the death of the last of the apostles, namely the apostle John, and the middle of the eighth century. In other words, those figures who were active in the life of the church between Ignatius of Antioch and Clement of Rome, who penned writings at the very beginning of the second century, and the Venerable Bede and John of Damascus, who stood at the close of antiquity and the onset of the Middle Ages. Far too many evangelicals in the modern day know next to nothing about these figures. I will never forget being asked to give a mini-history conference at a church in southern Ontario. I suggested three talks on three figures from Latin-speaking North Africa: Perpetua, Cyprian, and Augustine. The leadership of the church came back to me seeking a different set of names, since they had never heard of the first two figures, and while they had heard of the third name, the famous bishop of Hippo Regius, they really knew nothing about him. I gave them another list of post-Reformation figures for the mini-conference, but privately thought that not knowing anything about these figures was possibly a very good reason to have a conference on them! I suspect that such ignorance is quite widespread among those who call themselves Evangelicals—hence the importance of this small series of studies on a select number of Church Fathers, to educate and inform God's people about their forebears in the faith.

Past appreciation for the Fathers

How different is the modern situation from the past, when many of our Evangelical and Reformed forebears knew and treasured the writings of the ancient church. The French Reformer John Calvin, for example, was ever a keen student of the Church Fathers. He did not always agree with them, even when it came to one of his favorite authors, namely, Augustine. But he was deeply aware of the value of knowing their thought and drawing upon the riches of their written works for elucidating the Christian faith in his own day. And in the seventeenth century, the Puritan theologian John Owen, rightly called the 'Calvin of England' by some of his contemporaries, was not slow to turn to the experience of the one he called 'holy Austin,' namely Augustine, to provide him with a pattern of God the Holy Spirit's work in conversion.

Yet again, when the Particular Baptist John Gill was faced with the anti-Trinitarianism of the Deist movement in the early eighteenth century, and other Protestant bodies—for instance, the English Presbyterians, the General Baptists, and large tracts of Anglicanism—were unable to retain a firm grasp on this utterly vital biblical doctrine, Gill turned to the Fathers to help him elucidate the biblical teaching regarding the blessed Trinity. Gill's example in this regard influenced other Baptists such as John Sutcliff, pastor of the Baptist cause in Olney, where John Newton also ministered. Sutcliff was so impressed by the *Letter* to *Diognetus*, which he wrongly supposed to have been written by Justin Martyr, that he translated it for *The Biblical Magazine*, a Calvinistic publication with a small circulation. He sent it to the editor of this periodical with the commendation that this second-century work is 'one of the most valuable pieces of ecclesiastical antiquity.'

One final caveat

One final word about the Fathers recommended in this small series of essays. The Fathers are not Scripture. They are senior conversation partners about Scripture and its meaning. We listen to them respectfully, but are not afraid to disagree when they err. As the Reformers rightly argued, the writings of the Fathers must be subject to Scripture. John Jewel, the Anglican apologist, put it well when he stated in 1562:

> But what say we of the fathers, Augustine, Ambrose, Jerome, Cyprian, etc.? What shall we think of them, or what account may we make of them? They be interpreters of the word of God. They were learned men, and learned fathers; the instruments of the mercy of God, and vessels full of grace. We despise them not, we read them, we reverence them, and give thanks unto God for them. They were witnesses unto the truth, they were worthy pillars and ornaments in the church of God. Yet may they not be compared with the word of God. We may not build upon them: we may not make them the foundation and warrant of our conscience: we may not put our trust in them. Our trust is in the name of the Lord.

Michael A. G. Haykin
The Southern Baptist Theological Seminary
Louisville, Kentucky

A CHRONOLOGY OF CYPRIAN'S LIFE

All dates in the book are A.D. unless otherwise stated. Many of these dates in this chronology are approximate.

200	Cyprian is born in Carthage
246	Cyprian is converted to Christianity. Writes *To Donatus* soon after
248	Cyprian is elevated to the bishopric
250	Emperor Decius pronounces his edict that every citizen must offer a sacrifice
250	Cyprian flees into hiding
251	Persecution ends and Cyprian returns to Carthage
253	A plague breaks out in Carthage and kills thousands
253	Valerian becomes emperor

257	Valerian gives the order for persecution
258	14 September, Cyprian is executed by the sword

PREFACE

Jesus said that 'unless a grain of wheat falls into the earth and dies, it remains alone; but if it dies, it bears much fruit.'[1] Tertullian, Cyprian's predecessor in Carthage, must have had this verse in mind when he famously stated, 'The blood of the martyrs is the seed [of the church].'[2] The blood-drenched soil of Carthage, from which Cyprian sprang, was fertile with the shed blood of dead saints. Around the time that Cyprian was born, a woman named Perpetua (d. 203) languished in prison awaiting her execution for the crime of *contumacia*, a Latin word that refers to an obstinate refusal to obey an authority, who in this case commanded her to renounce her faith. During the trial she was repeatedly asked to deny Christ, even at the tearful behest of her father,[3] but her reply never wavered: *Christiana sum*, that is, 'I

---

1   John 12:24, NASB.
2   Tertullian, *Apology* 50, 'Of the church', is often added to this phrase. It does not appear in the original text, but does communicate the sentiment.
3   Candida Moss remarks on the seriousness of disobeying one's father in such a culture: 'The female martyr's death is often tied to the idea of rejecting one's family' ('Blood Ties: Martyrdom, Motherhood, and Family in the Passion of Perpetua and Felicity,' in *Women Seeking the Divine: Interdisciplinary Approaches*, ed. Stephen

am a Christian.'[4] Perpetua, the young mother of a nursing infant and daughter of a well-to-do patrician, clung to her faith despite severe threats, and she was martyred along with her friends in the coliseum in Carthage. As Jesus promised, the grains of wheat planted in their deaths did not remain alone; they produced manifold fruit, none more important than Cyprian, who would in turn fall into the earth as a seed, so that he too could bear much fruit in his death.

Persecution for one's faith was not new in Cyprian's day, nor did it end when Constantine legalized Christianity. Persecution is a peculiar means by which God has chosen to grow His church throughout the ages. As I write this, Islamic militants are sweeping through Iraq and Syria, forcing ancient pockets of Christians either to flee or face martyrdom. Many who have fled are dying of starvation and many who remain are enduring horrendous deaths. One Christian man was forced to recite the *shahada* ('Allah is God and Mohammed is his prophet'), and even after he capitulated, the terrorists decapitated him. When persecution abates, and it always does, those who are left will have to answer difficult questions. What about Christians who spoke the *shahada* in a moment of fear and panic? Can those who denied Christ be readmitted to the church? What about Christians who pretended to be Muslims to avoid mistreatment? Can they come back to the church and pretend as though nothing ever happened? If they are allowed back into the fold, should there be any prerequisite before rejoining? If it is not Iraq or Syria, it will be another persecution somewhere else. The church of Jesus Christ is promised existence through tribulation.[5] Perhaps no voice will be as important as Cyprian's in the coming days, who had to face these same questions when

---

    P. Ahearne-Kroll, James A. Kelhoffer, and Paul A. Holloway [Tübingen: Mohr Siebeck, 2010], p. 189).

4   *The Passion of S. Perpetua*, ed. J. Armitage Robinson, Texts and Studies 1.2 (Eugene, OR: Wipf and Stock, 1891), p. 6.

5   John 15:18-20.

persecution threatened the church in the middle of the third century, and who furnished the church with the first answers to these difficult problems.

Another world crisis draws Cyprian to the fore. When I first started writing this, the deadly Ebola virus was decimating much of West Africa and had spread to America, though the outbreak is contained for now. In all the hysteria and panic, many, including Christians, were more concerned with quarantine than compassion. After the persecution of Decius, which will be addressed in the following pages, a great disease and famine broke out in northern Africa. Instead of retreating from the city, Cyprian and other Christians entered into the misery, caring for the sick, and exposing themselves to disease and death. The church of today can learn from this too. Whether it is Ebola, AIDS, or an unknown disease we will meet in the future, the church has the responsibility to enter into the world's pain with the gospel, setting aside the cares of this temporal world for the heavenly city. Until Christ returns, the world will be subject to plagues and persecutions, but these are precisely the arenas in which the love of Christ and the compassion of the church are most palpably demonstrated.

Thus, Cyprian of Carthage has much to offer Christians in the present day. He converted to Christianity later in life, ministered for a decade, faced multiple trials, and was martyred. But in that brief window of ministry, Cyprian was able to navigate the church through turbulent waters like a skilled sailor, which was remarkable given his brief time as a deckhand before promoting to captain. Almost all of his contributions centered on the importance of the church. Unlike those in the second century who wrote apologies of the Christian faith, and unlike those in the fourth century who wrote tractates on the Trinity, Cyprian was forced in the third century to fight a different battle, summed up in a simple question: what is the church? Persecution sent a seismic shock through the church, causing confusion and factions, but Cyprian maintained that Christ's seamless garment, representative of the church, should not be rent.[6] Nothing challenges the structure and authority of the church quite like persecution. Although it might take a while for physical persecution to infiltrate the West, it is no secret that the church's influence is eroding. The coming storm for evangelicals will be centered on the nature of the church and Cyprian provides substantial answers to the questions that will be asked. The gathering clouds of this storm can be frightening given the current state of ecclesiology, the doctrine of the church, in evangelicalism.

Evangelicals have notoriously been faulted for weak ecclesiology, especially since the evangelical movement incorporates many streams of polity.[7] For the sake of agreement on the essentials, evangelicals of one denomination have been willing to lock arms with evangelicals of other denominations that have vastly different understandings of the church. Michael Bird has taken to task this weakness, calling it 'ecclesiology-lite'. He writes, 'While this ecclesiology-lite approach leads to wonderful opportunities to work with other Christians without denominational interference, it can also lead to a disinterest in

---

6   Cyprian, *On the Unity of the Church* 7-8.

7   Brad Harper and Paul Louis Metzger argue, 'Instead of saying that evangelicals don't have an ecclesiology, it may be better to say that the majority of evangelicals have a weak ecclesiology. A weak ecclesiology is characterized by a minimalist view of God's role for the church in his plan of salvation. It tends to emphasize the individual Christian and sees the church as existing primarily to nurture the believer. A weak ecclesiology also highlights the "universal" and "invisible" nature of the church to the detriment of the "local" and "visible" church' (Brad Harper and Paul Louis Metzger, *Exploring Ecclesiology: An Evangelical and Ecumenical Introduction* [Grand Rapids: Brazos Press, 2009], p. 295 n. 11). See also Bruce Hindmarsh, "Is Evangelical Ecclesiology an Oxymoron?" in *Evangelical Ecclesiology: Reality or Illusion?* ed. John G. Stackhouse Jr. (Grand Rapids: Baker Academic, 2003), pp. 15-37. The good news is that there is a renewal of interest in ecclesiology among evangelicals, most recently demonstrated in the work by Gregg Allison, *Sojourners and Strangers* (Foundations of Evangelical Theology; Wheaton: Crossway, 2012). Still, Cyprian can be of use as evangelicals are forced to ask difficult questions about the nature of the church in a society that has become secular.

the structure, organization, and visibility of the church.'[8] This disregard for Christ's bride would have amazed Cyprian, since it was he who emphasized, 'There is no salvation outside of the church,' and, 'You cannot have God as your Father if you do not have the church as Mother.' Cyprian would not allow a loose connection to the church. The church is integral to personal salvation.

The purpose of this book is twofold. The first aim is to introduce Cyprian to a new generation of Christians. Of all the illustrious figures of the early church, Cyprian often slips between the cracks. Evangelicals in particular have all but forgotten Cyprian. If you pick up a survey of the Fathers written by an evangelical, you are unlikely to find an extended treatment of Cyprian. Quite frankly, evangelicals are unsure of what to do with Cyprian because he seems too Roman Catholic. When I mentioned to a senior scholar that I was writing a book on Cyprian he shook his head in disbelief. 'Cyprian!' he exclaimed. 'I hate Cyprian!' This professor had communicated a shared belief among evangelicals, namely: What hath evangelicals to do with Cyprian? In the course of this book I hope to demonstrate that he is not as Catholic as many have thought—in the modern sense of Roman Catholic.

The second aim of this book is to demonstrate the significance of Cyprian for today. The goal of this series on the Fathers is to provide a *ressourcement*, or a revisiting of the piety and theology of the past for help in the present.[9] Increasingly our world looks more like Cyprian's world. For more than a millennium and a half the tides of Christian culture have risen, giving a Christian identity to the western world, for the good and the bad. But for the first time since Constantine, the high tides have begun

---

8   Michael Bird, *Evangelical Theology: A Biblical and Systematic Introduction* (Grand Rapids: Zondervan, 2013), p. 701.

9   Michael Haykin set the tone for this in his inaugural volume *Patrick: His Life and Impact* (Ross-shire, Scotland: Christian Focus, 2014), p. 19.

to ebb, and we are talking about the west as post-Christian.[10] In this new epoch, pluralism, subjective morality, and tolerance stand as the supreme virtues.[11] When we look back in time, we see that the third century was very similar to the present. The Romans allowed a plurality of religious beliefs, possessed subjective morality regarding sexual ethics, and even tolerated a broad spectrum of beliefs and practices, so long as an individual was willing to nod to the state religion. In many ways we find ourselves once more in pagan society. What we need are pastors and church members who can apply old truths to new times.

One final word is in order. I quote Cyprian at length because I want this book to be inspirational and not just informative.[12] The Fathers wrote in large measure to inspire deeper faith. To read them without this motive is to misread them entirely. My hope is that you will be struck by the sincerity of faith, the poignancy of the rhetoric, and the devotion unto death that accentuate all of Cyprian's writings.

Acknowledgments

In 2008 I underwent a period of personal angst as I contemplated where I wanted to complete my doctoral studies. Confident that the Lord was calling me to pursue a higher degree, I went about

---

10 The emphasis here is on the west. Christianity is experiencing tremendous growth in the southern and eastern hemispheres, which will soon be home to the majority of the world's Christians. See Philip Jenkins, *The Next Christendom: The Coming of Global Christianity*, 3rd ed. (New York: Oxford University Press, 2011).

11 See D. A. Carson's, *The Intolerance of Tolerance* (Grand Rapids, Eerdmans, 2012).

12 Important note to the reader: I have chosen to quote from a recent compilation of Cyprian's works, *The Complete Works of Saint Cyprian of Carthage*, ed. Phillip Campbell (Merchantville, N.J.: Evolution Publishing, 2013). The reason I use this volume is so that those wishing to study Cyprian can find all of his works combined in this one, readable book. The translation is virtually identical to the ANF (Ante-Nicene Fathers) except that the language has often been updated (e.g. removal of 'thou,' etc.), making the passages smoother for the modern reader. This volume also follows the ordering of the *Letters* of the ANF (after Jacques Paul Migne), which is out of sync with the Oxford edition of the *Letters*. See especially, G. W. Clarke, *The Letters of St. Cyprian of Carthage*, 4 vols. (New York: Newman Press, 1984). Also, citations from Church Fathers unaccompanied by a reference come from the ANF and NPNF (Nicene and Post-Nicene Fathers).

visiting several schools and speaking with different professors, trying to finalize a decision. As providence would have it, I attended the North American Patristics Society meeting that year and had the pleasure of meeting Dr. D. Jeffrey Bingham. I laid out the options as I saw them and in the course of my ramblings he stopped me and gave me some of the best advice I have ever received: 'Stop looking at schools and pick a supervisor. You will be molded by his or her character.' Immediately, all the questions about where I would attend, which had been swirling about endlessly in my mind, evaporated. I knew in that moment that I wanted to study under Michael Haykin, who had graciously extended to me an invitation to study under him. I can only hope that my character has been, and is continuing to be, influenced by him.

Were it not for him, I would not be contributing a volume in this series. Just hours before I defended my dissertation, Dr. Haykin took me to lunch (as he had so many times before) and asked if I would write on a Father. After less than a second I blurted out that I would. The fact that he would even consider me is an honor I do not take lightly. His guidance as a *Doktorvater* and his pastoral wisdom as a mentor sharpened my mind and warmed my heart. Only heaven knows the depth of his impact on my life.

I wrote the bulk of this book while serving as Pastor of Smithland First Baptist Church. The fine people there believed it was part of their broader ministry to afford me the time it takes to research and write—I am grateful beyond words for a congregation that understood this. I also want to express my deepest appreciation to Phoenix Seminary. Those at the Seminary have treated me kindly and have provided me with everything I needed to complete this book, especially the Phoenix Seminary Library staff—Doug Olbert, Jim Santeford, and Mitch Miller—and my colleagues John Meade and John DelHousaye who read portions of the manuscript and offered continual encouragement. Matt Crawford, already an established Patristics scholar, read the entire manuscript in a pinch and has saved me from errors in numerous places and gave insightful feedback. Shawn Wilhite took time away from his busy schedule to help a friend. I am deeply impressed by him, and I am excited to see how God will use him to advance our knowledge of early Christianity.

I dedicate this book to my children, Jameson and Natalie, because they are a great joy, even in the challenging toddler years! I hope Cyprian's passion for Christ will fill their hearts as they grow. In the last year of writing we suffered the loss of three second-trimester miscarriages, and I would feel remiss not to mention Finley, Hazel, and Beckett here too, whom we deeply loved. My wife deserves the most honor. I am sure there was a part of her that thought that once school was finished, those long hours tucked away in the study were behind us. But she never complained. She just continued to serve me and our family selflessly. 'An excellent wife, who can find?' (Prov. 31:10). Me, by God's grace!

Brian J. Arnold
Phoenix, Arizona
Summer, 2017

1

Cyprian of Carthage

Carthage

Perched on the northernmost tip of Africa, situated on the southwest coast of the Gulf of Tunis (modern-day Tunisia), Carthage was the most significant city of Roman Africa. The city was originally settled by Phoenicians in the ninth century B.C. and it was the Phoenician culture and religious practices that shaped Carthage for centuries, even to Cyprian's day.[1] This city was strategic for Rome, one of the great seaports of North Africa. But Carthage had not always belonged to Rome; it was once an independent nation, and Rome's bitter foe.

The history of Rome is the story of conquest, as she sought to extend her borders around the Mediterranean Sea, or as the Romans narcissistically called it, *Mare Nostrum*—'our sea'. Hungry for expansion, Rome conquered Greece in the east (146 B.C. and Gaul (modern-day France) in the west (51 B.C.). They would also venture north to Britannia (modern-day Britain) in 43, placing the Roman standard wherever their foot trod. But it was Carthage in the south that stood between Rome and world domination, the fiercest superpower that needed to be

---

1 For a helpful background on Carthage, see especially Serge Lancel, *Carthage: A History*, trans. Antonia Nevill (Oxford: Blackwell, 1995). Even the name Carthage comes from the Phoenician Kart-Hadasht, meaning 'new city'.

toppled.² The Roman poet Virgil epitomized Carthage as 'a rich city trained and fierce in war'.³

The history between Rome and Carthage was bloody. Nearly five hundred years before Cyprian's birth, Rome invaded Carthage for what would be known as the Punic wars,⁴ a series of three wars that would last over a century, after which Rome finally subdued her old enemy and assimilated Carthage into the empire (146 B.C.) For years, though, the conflict seemed nothing more than an endless tug-of-war, with each side prematurely declaring victory, while their foe, wounded for the moment, recuperated their strength and then regained the upper hand. Polybius called the First Punic War (264–241 B.C.) a 'boxing match' as though each side had met 'to fight for a prize' in a war filled with 'sorties and counter-attacks'⁵ The tale as Polybius recounts it is almost comical at times. Just when certain and total victory seemed within reach, a strange bit of providence (attributed loosely to the god Fortune in his writings) would turn the tide away from victory for either side.⁶ At the time of the initial engagement, the 'Carthaginians . . . enjoyed the complete mastery of the sea,'⁷ but Rome's military might was

---

2   Even though Rome still had much of the world to conquer after the century long war with Carthage, there was no enemy quite as worthy. Victory in northern Africa ensured global domination for Rome. However, had Rome lost, western civilization would be very different. Polybius provides an interesting 'what if' of history, saying, 'There are excellent reasons, therefore, for admiring Hannibal's ability in these respects, and we can say with confidence that if only he had subdued other parts of the world first and finished with the Romans, not one of his projects would have eluded him' (*The Rise of the Roman Empire* 11.19). But as John Faulkner has said, 'If there had to be a war between Carthage and Rome, it was for the infinite gain of the world that Rome was conqueror' (*Cyprian: the Churchman* [Cincinnati: Jennings and Graham, 1906], p. 15).

3   Virgil, *Aeneid* 1.13, trans. Robert Fagles (New York: Penguin, 2006), p. 48.

4   They were called the Punic Wars after the Latin word *Punicus*, meaning 'Carthaginian'. reminiscent of the Phoenician heritage of Carthage.

5   Polybius, *The Rise of the Roman Empire* 1.57.

6   Polybius, *The Rise of the Roman Empire* 1.58.

7   Polybius, *The Rise of the Roman Empire* 1.55.

on the rise, and they would win the day. After two devastating defeats, the Romans rebuilt their navy and finally were able to overtake the Carthaginians. The First Punic War was over after decades of stalemate.

But Carthage would not stay down for long. The Second Punic War (218-203 B.C.) featured epic scenes of Hannibal crossing the Alps with elephants, the Carthaginian's secret weapon. He surprised the Romans and won several crushing defeats. However, the cold mountain air killed off much of his cavalry, and so he was forced to stop short of Rome. The Carthaginians eventually retreated to North Africa and Scipio Africanus subsequently defeated Hannibal at the Battle of Zama in 202 B.C.

Carthage's military was decimated after these wars, but fifty years later they were able to muster an army one last time. As long as Carthage was breathing, Rome thought they had something to fear, which prompted Cato the Elder to pronounce, *Carthago delenda est*, that is, 'Carthage must be destroyed'.[8] Under the command of Scipio Aemilianus, who was also known as Scipio Africanus the Younger, Rome finally sacked Carthage, looting what they could before leveling the city. Rome's vitriolic hatred of Carthage ran so deep that a rumor started (the origins of which trace to the nineteenth century), that Rome salted the fields of Carthage so that they would be forever infertile.[9]

---

8 Although these words from Cato were not recorded for two hundred years after Carthage was destroyed, Cato allegedly ended every speech at the Senate with this statement. See Richard Miles, *Carthage Must be Destroyed: The Rise and Fall of an Ancient Civilization* (New York: Penguin, 2010), p. 336. Pliny the Younger appears to be the first to place these words on Cato's tongue. See Pliny, *Natural History* 15.74-5.

9 See R. T. Ridley, 'To be Taken with a Pinch of Salt: The Destruction of Carthage,' *Classical Philology* 81 (1986) pp. 140-46. The historian looks in vain for the reference of such an action, even though much of Polybius's work is lost. Rome rarely desecrated the lands they conquered. They were not trying simply to destroy an enemy; rather, they were on conquest to expand their boundaries and assimilate their enemies into the Republic. It would have been foolish to ruin the land and thus the economy of Carthage.

Worse than the prospect of salting the fields, however, was a curse that Scipio Aemilianus allegedly chanted over Carthage that forbade the rebuilding of the city.[10] Angered by the century-long war and wanting to ensure that there was not going to be a Fourth Punic war, he spoke a curse that would haunt the city even until Cyprian's day. This was no trivial curse. As Allen Brent observes, 'To curse . . . a territory meant that there could be no sacralized space.'[11] The political sphere was so intertwined with the spiritual that a curse invoking the gods affected politics, economic growth, and the religious atmosphere. Again, Brent identifies the predicament, saying, 'at its heart the foundation of Roman Carthage involved a metaphysical problem: the removal of the curse of Scipio'.[12] The mix of politics and religion would be devastating for the Christian Church, as we shall soon see.

Carthage began to be settled by Romans around 110 B.C. when Roman general Marius gave land to military veterans, but it was not until Augustus triumphed over Marc Antony that major renovations got underway.[13] Like the legendary phoenix, Carthage was raised from her ashes and restored to her former glory, though this time under the shadow of the Roman Eagle. Merdinger notes, 'During the following decade, engineers reconfigured the old Punic capital into an orderly Roman city replete with a theater, odeon, baths, amphitheater, and an aqueduct stretching 120 km from mountain headwater.'[14] Carthage was a fully incorporated Roman city and as such, the city began to

---

10 There is some debate as to the validity of this account. Early historians do not make mention of this curse. However, their works are fragmentary enough in certain sections where the curse could likely have been recorded.

11 Allen Brent, *Cyprian and Roman Carthage* (Cambridge: Cambridge University Press, 2010), p. 29.

12 Brent, *Cyprian and Roman Carthage*, p. 29.

13 Jane Merdinger, 'Roman North Africa,' in *Early Christianity in Contexts: An Exploration across Cultures and Continents*, ed. William Tabbernee (Grand Rapids: Baker Academic, 2014), p. 228.

14 Merdinger, 'Roman North Africa,' p. 228.

take on Roman characteristics even though, as it was in many instances, cities retained many of their religious and cultural practices. Romans were skilled in the art of governance in this way, often allowing the conquered to keep their religious beliefs and practices intact. Virgil says, 'But you, Roman, remember, rule with all your power the peoples of the earth—these will be your arts: to put your stamp on the works and ways of peace, to spare the defeated, break the proud in war.'[15] This even went for the hated city of Carthage.

By Cyprian's day, the religious atmosphere was eclectic, including a combination of Roman superstition (the use of auguries), old Phoenician gods (Baal), the Roman Pantheon (Jupiter and the like), emperor worship (burning incense to his *genius*), mystery religions from the East (especially, Isis, Sarapis, and Cybele),[16] a small Jewish presence, and a growing Christian population.[17] It was, to say the least, an amalgam of religious pluralism.[18] For many people, Christians included, religion was a potpourri of personal taste, adding this tradition or subtracting that rite, and this did not seem to bother the populace. However, as Christianity grew and as theology was developed and articulated, strict monotheism and an abandonment of ancient religious practices became a growing concern for Romans.

---

15 Virgil, *Aeneid* 6.850-53, trans. Robert Fagles, 210.

16 Merdinger notes the influx of Greek mystery cults by the fourth century B.C. 'The Greek deities Kore and Demeter had become popular at Carthage, as well as Isis and Sarapis from Egypt, and the Great Mother, Cybele, from Syria' (Merdinger, 'Roman North Africa,' p. 226).

17 Merdinger's analysis of the religious milieu in which Christianity was birthed is helpful, especially for understanding the rigidity that would come to mark Christianity in North Africa. She writes, 'Judaism remained the most potent element in the new faith, but indigenous Berber cults, harsh Punic rites, punctilious Greco-Roman ceremonies, and exuberant Eastern rituals would stamp North African Christianity with a rigorism peculiarly its own' (Merdinger, 'Roman North Africa,' pp. 223-4).

18 For a helpful introduction to various religious influences in the early church, see Hans Josef Klauck, *The Religious Context of Early Christianity: A Guide to Graeco-Roman Religions* (Minneapolis: Fortress Press, 2003).

Christians taught not only that there is only one God, but that every person must submit to this God. It did not take long for the church to attract attention, but not the attention she was hoping for.

The first glimpse of Christianity in North Africa comes in the martyrdom account known as the *Acts of the Scillitan Martyrs*, a group of seven men and five women put to death in Carthage on 17 July 180. Christianity must have been established for some time before 180, since Christianity was large enough to gain notice from imperial authorities to warrant execution. Likely Christianity washed up on Carthage's shore from a visitor or immigrant who had come to faith in another city, since the Carthaginian church could boast no apostolic sponsorship. By all estimations, the church was planted deeply and spread widely along the North African coast. Even as Islam conquered North Africa with lightning speed in the seventh century, Christianity spread, though through very different means, along the southern Mediterranean with surprising alacrity.

In time, the North African church became the intellectual hub of the church during the Patristic period, boasting the towering figures of Tertullian, Cyprian, and Augustine among many others.[19] The church came to life by the death of those unwilling to bow the knee to Caesar. Their blood sustained the church through one of the bleakest times in world history, which brings us to the dark days of the third century.

Cyprian's Carthage

At the turn of the third century, Rome was entering a period of great unrest.[20] Known as the 'age of anxiety', the crisis of the

---

[19] Hans von Campenhausen tells the sad story of North African Christianity in these words: 'The African church [through Tertullian, Cyprian, and Augustine] led the West intellectually for centuries; and only at her decline in the turmoils of the Arab conquest did she become silent forever.' (*The Fathers of the Latin Church*, trans. Manfred Hoffman [Stanford, California: Stanford University Press, 1964], p. 36).

[20] For a good overview, see Alan K. Bowman, *The Cambridge Ancient History: The Crisis*

third century was detrimental to the empire, as 'indicated by a constant and rapid turnover of emperors between 235 and 284, by near-continuous warfare, internal and external, combined with the total collapse of the silver currency'.[21] Rome's frontiers were challenged by Goths and Sassanids, leadership turned over frequently, and resources were siphoned off from the periphery of the empire into Rome, as can be seen in the lack of new architecture which had previously been on the rise.[22] From Commodus (d. 192) to Constantine (d. 337), Rome would know more than thirty emperors, as the greatest threats to security came from within the ranks. Generals marched into Rome with their legions, assassinated the reigning Caesar, and assumed the throne, creating uncertainty and instability.

This period of tumult came on the heels of the second century, a golden age if ever there was one. Edward Gibbon, author of the classic *Decline and Fall of the Roman Empire*, opened his *magnum opus* by hailing the accomplishments of Rome in the second century.

> In the second century of the Christian era, the Empire of Rome comprehended the fairest part of the earth, and the most civilized portion of mankind. The frontiers of that extensive monarchy were guarded by ancient renown and disciplined valour. The gentle but powerful influence of laws and manners had gradually cemented the union of the provinces. Their peaceful inhabitants enjoyed and abused the advantages of wealth and luxury.[23]

---

of Empire, A.D. 193–337 (Cambridge: Cambridge University Press, 2005).

21 Averil Cameron, *The Later Roman Empire A.D. 284–430* (Cambridge, MA: Harvard University Press, 1993), p. 3. See also A. R. Birley, 'The Third Century Crisis,' *Bulletin of the John Rylands Library* 58 (1976): pp. 253–81.

22 W. H. C. Frend, *The Rise of Christianity* (Philadelphia: Fortress Press, 1984), p. 308.

23 Edward Gibbon, *The Decline and Fall of the Roman Empire* (New York: Penguin, 1994), p. 31. Gibbon was no friend to Christianity. His narrative links the destruction of Rome to the rise of Christianity (and barbarism), and the heroes of the faith are often cast as villains in his tale. Others today make similar claims. See for instance, Charles Freeman, *The Closing of the Western Mind: The Rise of Faith and the*

This impressive empire that spanned 'the fairest part of the earth' transferred hands from capable emperors like Trajan, Hadrian, and Marcus Aurelius to emperors such as Gordian I, Balbinus, and Pupienus, all who served in 238, causing the entire Mediterranean world to spiral downward into chaos and darkness. Rome began to recover when Diocletian in the 280s made substantial administrative reforms. He divided the empire in half, east and west, and installed two *Augusti*, who ruled as emperors, and two *Caesares*, who served as second in command. This arrangement was called the Tetrarchy.

It is a matter of intense debate among Roman historians as to why Rome did not entirely implode in the third century. Again, Gibbon claims, 'The whole period was one uninterrupted series of confusion and calamity.'[24] So uncertain were those days that little record from secular authors exists. Anthony Birley, commenting on the decay of Rome and the lack of literature from this era, states that the sources are 'meager in the extreme'.[25] Maurice Bévenot eloquently speaks of the importance of Cyprian's writings for understanding this period: 'St. Cyprian's writings provide a leisured oasis in the otherwise almost desert landscape of third-century Western Christendom.'[26] Historians, then, are left to stitch together the fragments found dispersed in Christian writings—Tertullian in the early third century, Cyprian in the middle, and Hilary at the beginning of the fourth century—regardless of the fact that these authors felt little need to document the happenings of the secular world.

There is, however, the occasional reference to the broader world that helps us shade in bits and pieces of the historical milieu. Strewn about Cyprian's writings, for instance, are hints

---

Fall of Reason (New York: Alfred A. Knopf, 2004).

24 Gibbon, *The Decline and Fall of the Roman Empire*, p. 268.

25 A.R. Birley, 'The Third-Century Crisis in the Roman Empire,' *Bulletin of the John Rylands University Library of Manchester* 58 (1976): p. 255.

26 Maurice Bévenot, 'Primatus Petro Datur: St. Cyprian on the Papacy,' *Journal of Theological Studies* n.s. 5, no. 1 (1954): p. 19.

as to what this period was like. In a letter to *Donatus* he describes the chaos of his day:

> Consider the roads blocked up by robbers, the seas beset with pirates, wars scattered all over the earth with the bloody horror of camps. The whole world is wet with mutual blood; and murder, which in the case of an individual is admitted to be a crime, is called a virtue when it is committed wholesale.[27]

His shock at the state of society came from the relative stability that existed in the previous centuries. Piracy on the Mediterranean, for instance, had virtually disappeared entirely since the time of Julius Caesar. In one of the best stories from antiquity, Caesar was himself a victim of piracy in his early twenties.[28] When his captors realized who it was they were holding hostage, they decided to ask for a ransom of twenty talents, to which Julius insisted they make it fifty. He even told them that they had better kill him for if they did not, he would return and butcher them all. Disbelieving the threats of an adolescent, the pirates accepted their ransom money and freed young Julius. True to his word, he amassed a fleet and hunted down the pirates, imprisoning them before crucifying them. This brought a virtual end to piracy in the Mediterranean for nearly three centuries, but now the empire was unraveling as pirates returned to the seas, robbers had returned to the roads, and murderers had risen to power.

The increase in crime was a symptom of political disease. With all the focus on Rome, there was less accountability in the outer recesses of the empire, including North Africa. This dark and uncertain hour called for decisive leaders in the church who could weather the storm and, like shepherds, guide their flocks through the valley of death's shadow. One such shepherd ruled in North Africa and gave leadership and vision to a church in confusion and chaos—Cyprian of Carthage.

---

27 Cyprian, *To Donatus* 6.

28 For this account see Plutarch, *Lives* 7.1.2.

From Roman aristocrat to Christian bishop

Thascius Caecilius Cyprianus, better known to us simply as Cyprian, was born into a pagan family of wealth and status sometime around 200.[29] We know frustratingly little of Cyprian's patrician lifestyle prior to his conversion, though some have suggested that he belonged to the ruling class, a curial or even a senatorial class.[30] Pontius, Cyprian's biographer intentionally left blank the early chapters of his life, choosing instead to begin with what really mattered: Cyprian's birth into the kingdom, around the year 246. Near the start of his brief biography, Pontius asks,

> At what point, then, shall I begin—from what direction shall I approach the description of his goodness, except from the

---

29 Michael Sage suggests that Cyprian's name has not been given correctly. Instead of Thascius Caecilius Cyprianus, his name was *Caecilius Cyprianus qui est Thascius*, that is, Caecilius Cyprianus who is (or as we might say, 'also known as') Thascius. It was common for Romans to have three names—a *nomen*, a *cognomen*, and a *praenomen*. The *nomen* referred to one's clan, the *praenomen* was used to differentiate people from within the clan, and the *cognomen* was the nickname. So, for instance, 'Cicero', the most famous of the Latin orators, was a *cognomen* that meant 'chickpea,' after an ancestor who had a wart on his nose! (See Anthony Everitt, *Cicero* [New York: Random House, 2003], p. 24). For a helpful and brief introduction to names in Roman culture see James Jeffers, *The Greco-Roman World of the New Testament Era: Exploring the Background of Early Christianity* (Downers Grove, IL: IVP Academic, 1999), pp. 202-4.

In this case, Michael Sage purports that Cyprian has a *nomen*, *cognomen*, and *agnomen*. Evidence for this comes to the surface in the way he is referred to in the edict that confiscates his property (*Letter* 66.4) and how he is addressed by the proconsul Galerius Maximus. It is telling that in *Letter* 66.4, the heading reads, *Cyprianus qui est Thascius* (Cyprian, who is Thascius). The *cognomen* Cyprianus is rare and yields little. Caecilius, the *nomen*, may have derived from the Caecilius who led Cyprian to faith (see below). The *agnomen*, Thascius, is just as obscure as the *cognomen*. Nothing in Cyprian's name unlocks his mysterious birth or pedigree. For a helpful discussion of this, see Michael Sage, *Cyprian* (Cambridge, MA: The Philadelphia Patristic Foundation, 1975), pp. 98-100.

30 Michael Sage, *Cyprian*, p. 106. Another facet of Cyprian's thought that might explain his background among the ruling class was his ecclesial developments around a diocese. Cyprian was innovative in his approach to polity and this might be a vestige from his former days of secular prominence, especially when it came to the similarity between the patron/client relationship and the bishop/congregation relationship. More will be said on this in chapter 3.

beginning of his faith and from his heavenly birth? Inasmuch as the doings of a man of God should not be reckoned from any point except from the time that he was born of God.[31]

There are those of us today who are desperate to know of Cyprian's upbringing and place in Roman society, but Pontius refused to satisfy the curiosity of future generations. Like the gospels, only that which was pertinent to Cyprian's renown was placed in the biography. Pontius may not give us much to go by, but there are clues sprinkled throughout his and Cyprian's writings that fill in the picture of his early years, not to mention the witness that we receive from the other Fathers.

If Gregory of Nazianzus is correct, Cyprian came from a senatorial family of wealth and he was given a first-rate education.[32] Gregory praises his hero in *Oration* 24:

> A man celebrated for his wealth, respected for his power, high-born (if the fact that he was a member and president of the senate best indicates his family's lineage), the flower of youthfulness, the monument of nature, a bastion of learning not only in philosophical studies but in the other disciplines and any of their divisions you will, so as to be admired more for the range of his learning than for his mastery of any one branch and more for his pre-eminence in each than for his encyclopedic knowledge of all; or, to make the distinction more clear, he was superior to some in the range of his learning, to others in his mastery of individual subjects, to still others in both, and to everyone in everything.[33]

---

31 Pontius, *The Life and Passion of Cyprian* 2.

32 To clear up any potential confusion, it is suggested in this chapter that Cyprian may have come from the curial class, a senatorial family, or that he was a magistrate. Everett Ferguson shows the similarity of these three positions, saying, 'There was also a local council (*curia*) of former magistrates (called *decuriones*) like the senate in Rome' (*Backgrounds of Early Christianity*, 3rd ed. [Grand Rapids: Eerdmans, 2003], p. 42). Pinpointing his class precisely is impossible.

33 Gregory Nazianzus, *Orations* 24.6, in *St. Gregory of Nazianzus: Select Orations*, trans. Martha Vinson (Fathers of the Church Patristic Series; Washington, DC: The Catholic University of America Press, 2003), p. 145.

Gregory must have received this information on Cyprian's family from tradition since the sources give away so little.

As for his remaining comments, Cyprian's own hand reveals the truth of this panegyric. That he came from wealth is clear from the outfits he wore to the fact that he sold off his wealth and donated it to the church upon his conversion. Regarding his eloquence and towering intellect, a cursory reading of his works display a sharp tongue and an encyclopedic knowledge of philosophy, theology, and law. Judging from the lofty praise he receives from the likes of Jerome and Augustine, Gregory's final comment of Cyprian's superiority 'to everyone in everything' does not seem overly exaggerated.[34]

For a young man born into a high station, an education in rhetoric would have been standard. Pontius confirms that Cyprian was devoted to the study of the *bonae artes*, that is, the 'good arts' or the liberal arts.[35] This led some of the later Fathers to suggest that Cyprian was a teacher of rhetoric, such as Jerome who mentions that Cyprian had this occupation prior to his conversion.[36] Modern commentators on Cyprian have almost uniformly suggested that Cyprian was a lawyer or advocate, because he uses language and ideas suggestive of a background in law, though this is entirely conjecture.[37] It is without doubt, however, that he was well-trained in the art of words.

Despite his schooling, Cyprian intentionally tried to tone down the rhetoric a few notches for the sake of the simpler-minded in the church, which would have included a majority of uneducated people. Ironically, even when Cyprian aimed at

---

34 Augustine calls Cyprian 'the most persuasive teacher'. See Augustine, *On Christian Doctrine* 2.40.

35 Pontius, *The Life and Passion of Cyprian* 2.1. Most biographical details come from Pontius's *Vita*, written after Cyprian's death, and Cyprian's letter *To Donatus*, which is likely the first writing we have from Cyprian's hand (c. 246).

36 See Jerome, *On Illustrious Men* 67.

37 See G. W. Clarke, 'The Secular Profession of St. Cyprian of Carthage,' *Latomus* 24 (1965): pp. 633–38.

simplicity in language, his words were clothed in splendor, as though he were unable to speak plainly no matter how hard he tried—his training and his gifting were too entrenched. Writing to Donatus he said,

> In courts of justice, in the public assembly, in political debate, a copious eloquence may be the glory of a voluble ambition; but in speaking of the Lord God, a chaste simplicity of expressions strives for the conviction of faith rather with the substance, than with the powers of eloquence. Therefore accept from me things, not clever but weighty words, decked up to charm a popular audience with cultivated rhetoric, but simple and fitted by their unvarnished truthfulness for the proclamation of the divine mercy.[38]

Cyprian's use of language is powerful. He employs illustrations, evokes emotion, engages polemically, and electrifies his reader for a response. He is familiar enough with the classics to cite them, but he does so sparingly. This is probably intentional—after his conversion, Scripture is his authority, not Cicero.[39] He benefits immensely from this training and yet he is in many ways the clichéd child of privilege who comes to reject his wealth and rank.

In this regard, and in many others, Cyprian is a man of paradox. For instance, he reacts against his wealth while also admitting the difficulty of giving it up, making his upbringing in privilege at once a catalyst and an obstacle to his conversion. At one point in his very brief biographical sketch, he rhetorically asks Donatus, 'He who has been glittering in gold and purple, and has been celebrated for his costly attire, when does he reduce himself to ordinary and simple clothing?'[40] While it might be tempting to think that gold was the extravagant accessory that

---

38 Cyprian, *To Donatus* 2.

39 Sage notes, 'While citations from the body of pagan literature abound in Tertullian, they are almost entirely absent from Cyprian's writings' (*Cyprian*, p. 135).

40 Cyprian, *To Donatus* 3.

was difficult to doff, in actuality it was the purple that would be harder to lay aside. Purple was a rare and expensive delicacy, harvested from thousands of murex shells in the vicinity of Tyre, each shell containing only a few drops.[41] Not only was purple a commodity that only the rich could afford, but it was also only worn by those of rank.[42] Given the description of purple and gold that Cyprian provides, it is possible that he has the *toga picta* in mind, a purple toga embroidered with gold. Magistrates and consuls, in addition to the emperor and senators, wore these togas, meaning that Cyprian was in fact near the top of the social strata

His ornate clothes were not the only difficult things to remove, it was the entire lifestyle that was nearly impossible to reject. 'When', asks Cyprian, 'does he learn thrift who has been used to liberal banquets and sumptuous feasts?'[43] Banquets were far more intricate and luxurious than we may think of them today. More than gorging and drunkenness, banquets were important social occasions that demonstrated a person's wealth and standing—the fancier the feast, the greater the prestige. Banquets might last the better part of a day and include different forms of entertainment, plenty of wine, and an abundance of food.[44] From liberal banquets to thrift, Cyprian would have to learn abstemiousness in diet and drink. He could not in good

---

41 See Charles Freeman, *The Closing of the Western Mind*, 83. Freeman notes that 1,200 murex shells were needed to produce just 1.6 grams of purple dye. For the Edict of Prices see Simon Corcoran, *The Empire of the Tetrarchs, Imperial Pronouncements and Government* A.D. *284–324*, rev. ed. (Oxford: Oxford University Press, 2000), pp. 205–233. Though much inflation had probably taken place during this unsettling century, it does give an idea of just how precious purple dye was. The Edict of Prices valued purple-dyed wool as equal to its weight in gold, 50,000 denarii a pound.

42 Nero banned the wearing of purple by anyone other than himself (Seutonius, *Nero* 32). And in the late Roman period, certain purple dyes were reserved for the emperor alone (see Alexandra Croom, *Roman Clothing and Fashion* [Gloucestershire: Amberley, 2010], np). Obviously this rule was relaxed between these times.

43 Cyprian, *To Donatus* 3.

44 See Everett Ferguson, *Backgrounds of Early Christianity*, p. 106.

conscience indulge in banquets and feasts while his Christian brothers and sisters lived in constant hunger. But he wrestled with whether or not he could give up his life of ease.

While reflecting on the difficulty of abandoning this former life of extravagance, he also can look back on those same banquets and remember the endless anxiety and vexation that accompanies wealth.

> Such a one enjoys no security either in his food or in his sleep. *In the midst of the banquet he sighs, although he drinks from a jeweled goblet*; and when his luxurious bed has enfolded his body, languid with feasting, in its yielding bosom, he lies wakeful in the midst of the down; nor does he perceive, poor wretch, that these things are merely gilded torments, that he is held in bondage by his gold, and that he is the slave of his luxury and wealth rather than their master.[45]

Wealth, which promises the end of worry, can actually produce greater disquiet in the soul. Years later Cyprian would say, 'How can they follow Christ, who are held back by the chain of their wealth? . . . They think that they possess, when they are rather possessed.'[46] He knew all too well the seductive nature of wealth. Even though he knew that wealth could not satisfy him, he nevertheless struggled to loosen wealth's grip that had seized his heart from birth. Becoming a Christian meant forsaking perhaps centuries of family wealth and position. Few are called to such a radical abandonment of worldly privilege. Cyprian succeeded where the rich young ruler failed, forfeiting his wealth to follow Jesus.

Conversion to Christ

It was against the backdrop of societal collapse and dissatisfaction with wealth that Cyprian dropped anchor in the harbor of

---

45 Cyprian, *To Donatus* 12, emphasis added.

46 Cyprian, *On the Lapsed* 12.

salvation, the only 'solid and firm and constant security'.[47] Jerome briefly recounts details of Cyprian's life and his conversion in his commentary on Jonah 3. 'Let us', says Jerome, 'place before ourselves the blessed Cyprian, who before was an advocate of idolatry, and attained such renown for his eloquence that he even taught oratory in Carthage. He heard at last the message of Jonah and having been converted to penitence he attained such courage that he proclaimed Christ publicly and bent his neck to the sword for his sake.'[48] How Cyprian came to be confronted with Jonah is a mystery. Did he stumble into a church and hear a sermon on Jonah? Did he come across a copy of Jonah, read it, and get converted? Likely it was a Christian who challenged him to read Scripture for himself; perhaps this is the service that Caecilius provided.

Pontius attributed Cyprian's conversion to Caecilius, a presbyter in the church at Carthage whom Cyprian would come to consider his 'parent in the faith,' who 'converted him from his worldly errors to the acknowledgment of the true divinity',[49] So close was their bond of affection that when Caecilius died, he entrusted the welfare of his family to Cyprian, who gladly took them under his wing. More than just taking his family in, Cyprian showed honor to his spiritual father by taking his surname, Caecilianus, as his own.

Cyprian recalled his coming to faith as a process that unfolded over a period of time. He gradually discovered that his entire life was vanity. We should not think of Cyprian's conversion as a pagan who was living for the world in one moment and gloriously converted in the next.[50] W. H. C. Frend observed that,

---

47 Cyprian, *To Donatus* 14.

48 Jerome, *Comm. Jon.* 3:6-9. For this translation, see Timothy Michael Hegedus, 'Jerome's Commentary on Jonah: Translation with introduction and critical notes' (MA Thesis, Wilfrid Laurier University, 1991), p. 54.

49 Pontius, *The Life and Passion of Cyprian* 4.

50 In a fascinating article, Edwina Murphy compares Cyprian's journey with that of Christian's in John Bunyan's *Pilgrim's Progress* ('Cyprian and *The Pilgrim's Progress,*'

'Becoming a Christian was often a matter of gradual decision, and eventually occurred when the convert was convinced that Christianity answered questions that pagan philosophies could not, and was a superior and more relevant faith.'[51] For this reason, Michael Sage cautions against taking Jerome seriously.[52] Sage tells the story of Cyprian's conversion as though there is a contradiction between a slow and a swift conversion. But there is no problem here. For years Cyprian wrestled with his growing disillusionment of the pagan world, and then, in an instant, he was converted. This is similar to Augustine who took a rather circuitous path to salvation, exploring Manichaeism and Neo-Platonism, until he too was converted one afternoon while hearing the children play outside of his garden.[53]

Of course, for Cyprian the primary actor in the story of his conversion was God.[54] Conversion to the true faith was much more than a simple change of the mind or a replacement of the affections. Something far more profound was happening in the inner man that could only be attributed to the workings of the

---

in *Beyond 400: Exploring Baptist Futures*, ed. David J. Cohen and Michael Parsons [Eugene, OR: Wipf and Stock, 2011], pp. 116-30). Both Cyprian and Bunyan 'knew what it was to live out faith in a hostile world, and they were alert to the dangers that must be faced and overcome in order to achieve the promised hope' (Idem., p. 119).

51 Frend, *The Rise of Christianity*, p. 312.

52 Sage, *Cyprian*, pp. 117-21.

53 In one of the more well-known conversion stories in history, Augustine tells of how he heard children outside playing a game of which he had never heard. The children were singing and as part of the chorus they sang, *Tolle, lege*, meaning, 'Take up and read.' He went at once to a copy of Paul's letter to the Romans that was open on his desk and read the first sentence on which his eyes fell—'Not in reveling and drunkenness, not in lust and wantonness, not in quarrels and rivalries. Rather, arm yourselves with the Lord Jesus Christ; spend no more thought on nature and nature's appetites.' Augustine was converted to Christianity in that moment, even though he had spent decades searching for the truth. (See *Confessions*, 8.12, trans. R. S. Pine-Coffin [New York: Penguin, 1961], pp. 177-78). Frend connects the salvation accounts of both Cyprian and Augustine, casting both stories as 'gloom and guilt' and a 'conversion [that] brought release' (Frend, *The Rise of Christianity*, p. 313).

54 Sage, *Cyprian*, pp. 129-31.

Holy Spirit. The old man of sin is removed and the person is regenerated through the baptism of water, during which time the Spirit is infused into the one who has faith.[55]

The greatest statement of his own conversion comes in his letter *To Donatus*, his first writing as a Christian (c. 246), sent to his friend Donatus about his newfound life. The purpose of the letter was ultimately an *apologia*, though there was also an evangelistic appeal, intended to convert others who remained in the clutches of sin.[56] Though lengthy, it is worth quoting in full since this section lays bare not only his own path to salvation, but also reveals a good deal about his view of salvation itself:

> For as I myself was held in bonds by the innumerable errors of my previous life, from which I did not believe that I could by possibility be delivered, so I was disposed to acquiesce in my clinging vices; and because I despaired of better things, I used to indulge my sins as if they were actually parts of me, and indigenous to me. But after that, by the help of the water of new birth, the stain of former years had been washed away, and a light from above, serene and pure, had been infused into my reconciled heart—after that, by the agency of the Spirit breathed from heaven, a second birth had restored me to a new man—then, in a wondrous manner, doubtful things at once began to assure themselves to me, hidden things to be revealed, dark things to be enlightened, what before had seemed difficult began to suggest a means of accomplishment, what had been thought impossible, to be capable of being achieved; so that I was enabled to acknowledge what previously, being born of the flesh, had been living in the practice of sins, was of the earth earthly, but had now begun to be of God, and was animated by the Spirit of holiness. You yourself assuredly know and recollect as well as I do what was taken away from us, and what was given to us by that death of evil, and that life of virtue. You yourself

---

55 Cyprian, *To Donatus* 14.

56 On the evangelistic purpose of the letter, see Sage, *Cyprian*, p. 128, and Allen Brent, *On the Church: Select Treatises* (Crestwood, N.Y.: St. Vladimir's Press, 2006), p. 47.

know this without my information. Anything like boasting in one's own praise is hateful, although we cannot in reality boast but only be grateful for whatever we do not ascribe to man's virtue but declare to be the gift of God; so that now we sin not is the beginning of the work of faith, whereas that we sinned before was the result of human error. All our power is of God; I say, of God. From Him we have life, from Him we have strength, by power derived and conceived from Him we do, while yet in the world, foreknow the indications of things to come.[57]

Cyprian was trapped in his former life of luxury and sin, which were in many ways one and the same for him. Sin clung to him, keeping him in bondage, so much so that it seemed to be part of his being. And so it was. But it was then that he experienced the new birth, the birth of which Jesus told Nicodemus two centuries before—'Truly, truly I say to you, unless one is born of water and the Spirit, he cannot enter the kingdom of God. That which is born of the flesh is flesh, and that which is born of the Spirit is spirit' (John 3:5-6). Like Nicodemus, Cyprian tripped over the idea that a person could be born again, or that one needed to be born again. In Cyprian's words, 'I used to regard it as a difficult matter . . . that a man should be capable of being born again—a truth which the divine mercy had announced for my salvation.'[58]

The role of the Holy Spirit in conversion is underappreciated in Cyprian scholarship, which would have profoundly bothered him, for Cyprian could not speak of his conversion without tracing the Spirit's involvement.[59] It was the reception of the Spirit

---

57 Cyprian, *To Donatus* 4.

58 Cyprian, *To Donatus* 3.

59 Michael Haykin has made a significant correction to this oversight. See Michael Haykin, 'The Holy Spirit in Cyprian's *To Donatus*,' *Evangelical Quarterly* 83.4 (2011): pp. 321-29. Haykin cites Adhemar d'Alès, *La théologie de Saint Cyprien* (Paris: G. Beauchesne, 1922), p. 11 and Manlio Simonetti, 'Il regresso della teologia dello Spirito santo in Occidente dopo Tertulliano,' *Augustinianum* 20 (1980): pp. 655-60 as examples of those who downplay Cyprian's pneumatology.

at baptism that transformed him into a new man. The water of baptism washed away the stains of former transgressions, but it was the Spirit that gave him 'a real measure of moral victory over his sins'.[60] Prior to conversion, sin was as natural as breathing for Cyprian. To part with sin would be like suicide since sin was so intertwined into his being, and he could think of no possible way to change. But after his conversion, sin suddenly lost its stranglehold and he experienced freedom through the indwelling of the Spirit of holiness. Before, he longed for the world; now he had new desires and leanings, desires that could have only come from God Himself.

This sudden change of life demonstrated to Cyprian that the Spirit cannot be tamed. He put it this way: 'The Spirit freely flowing forth is restrained by no limits, is checked by no closed barriers within certain bounded spaces.'[61] Haykin avers that 'the key to understanding this passage is the pneumatological affirmation that there is no limit to the Spirit's sovereign and free presence'.[62] Again, borrowing from the idea of Jesus in John 3, the Spirit is like that wind that blows wherever it wants, whenever it wants. It comes and goes and no one can contain it. Cyprian had firsthand experience of the Spirit's effects, having been drastically renewed and changed. For our part, Cyprian says, we must desperately desire the Spirit to move in us. Cyprian entices us, saying, 'Let our heart only be thirsty, and be ready to receive: in the degree in which we bring to it a capacious faith, in that measure we draw from it an overflowing grace.'[63]

In addition to his rich pneumatology, another striking feature of Cyprian's reflection on his conversion is just how monergistic he was in his theology. That is, God, and God alone, is the author of salvation. 'All our power is of God; I say,

---

60   Michael Haykin, 'The Holy Spirit in Cyprian's *To Donatus*,' p. 323.

61   Cyprian, *To Donatus* 5.

62   Michael Haykin, 'The Holy Spirit in Cyprian's *To Donatus*,' p. 325.

63   Cyprian, *To Donatus* 5.

of God,' Cyprian uttered in total amazement.[64] All the power Cyprian had in his former life, all the clients he had as a patron, all the authority he had to rule, were as nothing in the presence of God who is truly omnipotent. God the almighty condescends to give salvation—it is not up to man even though it is available to every person. Salvation is 'a gratuitous gift from God, and it is accessible to all'.[65] Cyprian recognized that salvation is a gift to be received by faith, despite his heavy emphasis on virtuous living. Virtue should result from salvation, but salvation itself is 'the gift of God' and cannot be 'ascribe[d] to man's virtue'.[66]

However long it may have taken Cyprian to inspect Christianity before finally adopting the faith as his own, his conversion brought about immediate and widespread change. He sold off his property and donated the proceeds to the church, though the church would buy back his estate and he would return to live there. He devoted himself to piety—prayer, fasting, and Scripture reading—and disentangled himself from public affairs. But his days as an anonymous Christian were short-lived.

Rise to Bishopric

When Bishop Donatus of Carthage died in 248, there were many questions about who would fill his chair (*cathedra*). As soon as Cyprian found out that his name was being considered, he 'humbly withdrew, giving place to men of older standing . . . thinking himself unworthy of a claim to so great honour'.[67] Cyprian knew that it was best to defer to men who had belonged to the household of faith longer than he had. But the populace could not be contained. Pontius records, 'A crowded fraternity was besieging the doors of the house, and throughout

---

64 Cyprian, *To Donatus* 4.

65 Cyprian, *To Donatus* 14.

66 Cyprian, *To Donatus* 4. A fuller discussion of Cyprian's view of salvation is given in chapter 4.

67 Pontius, *The Life and Passion of Cyprian* 5.

all the avenues of access an anxious love was circulating.'[68] The people pressed in on every side, shouted his name for bishop, and would not leave until they got what they wanted.[69]

So, within two years of his conversion Cyprian became the bishop of Carthage (c. 248), one of the more important seats in ancient Christianity, bypassing the normal rungs on the ecclesial ladder. Not surprisingly, Cyprian's lightning elevation was met with a good deal of opposition. Even the Roman Tacitus understood people's proclivity for jealousy, saying, 'Such is the nature of the human mind, disposed at all times to behold with jealousy the sudden elevation of new men, and to demand, that he, who has been known in an humble station should know how to rise in the world with temper and modest dignity.'[70] The challenge was that Cyprian came from anything but a humble station, even though his recent conversion should have been interpreted in such a way. In the household of faith, a former life of poverty or wealth, homelessness or extravagance, whether slave or owner, should provide equal footing. Cyprian's previous life as a statesman should not have influenced the church to make him a bishop, but it was impossible for those in Carthage to overlook Cyprian and the prestige he could bring the church. The Christians believed that his former life would give them special privilege in society and they could boast that their bishop already had great renown in the city.

Cyprian's critics were not without scriptural grounds to cast doubt on his candidacy for bishop. The apostle Paul had warned against raising a man to the role of overseer before his life displayed mature virtue. In a response that was part apologetic

---

68 Pontius, *The Life and Passion of Cyprian* 5.

69 In the early Patristic era, it was common to elect a bishop by acclamation, that is, by the overwhelming will and decree of the people. Ambrose became bishop of Milan under very similar circumstances, but not long after Ambrose was installed as bishop this practice was abandoned because of the potential for abuse.

70 Tacitus, *Historical Works*, ed. E. H. Blakeney (London: J. M. Dent & sons, 1917), 2:89.

and part admiration, Pontius gave a defence for Cyprian's elevation to the episcopacy as a young believer. He says,

> No one reaps immediately upon his sowing; no one presses out the vintage harvest from the trenches just formed; no one ever yet sought for ripened fruit from newly planted slips. But in [Cyprian] all incredible things concurred. In him the threshing preceded . . . sowing, the vintage the shoots, the fruit the root.[71]

From Pontius's perspective, Cyprian was unique in his conversion. He scaled the heights of Christian maturity almost simultaneously to his conversion by plumbing the depths of Christian theology, memorizing large sections of Scripture, and leading the way in the care of the poor. Fully aware of Paul's restrictions of placing a neophyte in leadership, Pontius says that Cyprian furnished an illustration that progress should be measured in faith and not in time.[72] Of this faith, Pontius declared, '[Cyprian] began with a faith as mature as that with which few perhaps have finished their course.'[73]

Soon after his rise to the episcopate, Cyprian's faith and leadership would be tested. By 250 the church would undergo her first empire-wide persecution under the Emperor Decius. Though we will take more time to examine this in the next chapter, it is important to note that Cyprian had very little time of peace before his ministry would be marked by suffering and controversy. Not long after the onset of persecution, Cyprian abandoned his post and fled into hiding, from where he could guide the church through the tumult. From his hiding place he began a vigorous letter-writing campaign to those left behind, particularly the presbyters who ruled in his stead. Though his friends and the congregations *en masse* followed him as their bishop, there were others who set themselves up in opposition

---

71   Pontius, *The Life and Passion of Cyprian* 2.

72   Pontius, *The Life and Passion of Cyprian* 3.

73   Pontius, *The Life and Passion of Cyprian* 3.

to him. Cyprian's decision to flee provided his opponents ammunition in their claim that Cyprian should never have been made a bishop.

The persecution lasted only about eighteen months but the damage was significant. The worst part was the confusion on how to handle the fractured church. Sitting in the same congregation were those who bore scars on their bodies from torture racks and those who capitulated to fear and sacrificed. Most noticeable were the empty seats where fathers and mothers, brothers and sisters once sat who gave up their earthly lives for their testimonies about Jesus. How should those who broke the ranks of faith be treated? Could those who sacrificed under the threat of punishment be allowed back into the church? If so, should they be required to demonstrate their contrition through penance? Questions like these divided many people in the church. Cyprian, as we shall see, suggested a middle position between grace and rigor.

Just as things were beginning to stabilize in the church, a horrific plague broke out across the empire, which has come to be known as the Plague of Cyprian. Pontius described the plague with these chilling words, 'There broke out a dreadful plague . . . carrying off day by day with abrupt attack numberless people, everyone from his own house . . . . There lay about the meanwhile, over the whole city, no longer bodies, but the carcasses of many, and, by the contemplation of a lot which in their turn would be theirs, demanded the pity of the passers-by for themselves.'[74] Bodies of the dead began to stack up in the streets because there were not enough people left to bury the remains. So they resorted to fire. According to Candida Moss, recent archeological discoveries have found bones covered in a layer of lime, an ancient form of disinfectant, alongside the site of an 'enormous bonfire, used to incinerate the remains of

---

74   Pontius, *Life and Passion of Cyprian* 9.

plague victims'.⁷⁵ Burning the bodies was the best they could do to prevent even more disease from the leftover bodies that littered the streets.

Modern scientists believe that the outbreak might have been smallpox, which also spread during the reign of Marcus Aurelius, who may himself have been a victim of the disease. Given Cyprian's description of the symptoms, this seems possible. Regardless of the specific pathogen, it was a devastating plague that ravaged the empire. At the height of the outbreak, an estimated five thousand people died daily in Rome, to say nothing of other major cities where the plague struck with greater brutality.

This pandemic was interpreted apocalyptically by early Christians and may have been part of the reason for the rapid spread of Christianity in the third century.⁷⁶ Christianity offered life after death. To those who contracted the disease, for whom death was imminent, Christianity provided a path to eternal serenity and release from pain. It was not just the promise of paradise or the thought the world was coming to an end in a most horrific way that led to exponential growth, it was mostly because the church stretched out a hand of compassion to those who were pitiable. As Rodney Stark puts it, 'In the midst of the squalor, misery, illness, and anonymity of ancient cities, Christianity provided an island of mercy and security.'⁷⁷ Christianity was the oasis of hope in a society that saw compassion as a weakness. The sick and dying did not think it weak at all, and this attracted the masses to faith in Jesus who called His followers to lay down their lives for the good of others (John 15:13).

---

75 Candida Moss, 'How an apocalyptic plague helped spread Christianity,' CNN (June 23, 2014), http://religion.blogs.cnn.com/2014/06/23/how-an-apocalyptic-plague-helped-christianity/, accessed March 3, 2015. Moss's article provides many of the helpful details in this section.

76 Candida Moss, 'How an apocalyptic plague helped spread Christianity.'

77 Rodney Stark, *The Triumph of Christianity* (New York: HarperOne 2011), p. 112.

Dionysius, Cyprian's counterpart in Alexandria, memorialized the heroic actions of Christians who sacrificed their own lives to plague in the service of others:

> Heedless of danger, they took charge of the sick, attending to their every need and ministering to them in Christ, and with them departed this life serenely happy; for they were infected by others with the disease, drawing on themselves the sickness of their neighbors and cheerfully accepting their pains. Many, in nursing and curing others, transferred their death to themselves and died in their stead . . . . The best of our brothers lost their lives in this manner, a number of presbyters, deacons, and laymen winning high commendation so that in death in this form, the result of great piety and strong faith, seems in every way the equal to martyrdom.[78]

Christians did not just offer their bodies in the amphitheater for refusing to sacrifice during the persecution, they also offered up their lives to care for the sick and dying during the plague.

It is in the arena of death that the Christian faith is put to its greatest test. Cyprian makes note of this when he writes to the faithful during the plague, imploring them to hold fast their faith. 'Unless the battle has preceded, there cannot be victory . . . . For the helmsman is recognized in the tempest; in the warfare the soldier is proved. It is wanton display when there is no danger. Struggle in adversity is the trial of the truth.'[79] Caring for the sick might cost a person her life, but Christian hope is in heaven, where she would be transported should she contract the disease and die. In short, the Christian cannot lose, since death itself is victory.

Cyprian put his wealth to good use during the epidemic as he was able to distribute money to those who were in dire need. He was not alone in his affection towards the sick. In

---

78 Dionysius, *Festal Letters*, in Eusebius, *The History of the Church* 7.22, as quoted in Rodney Stark, *Triumph of Christianity*, p. 117.

79 Cyprian, *On Mortality* 12.

droves Christians entered into the misery with mercy, even the presbyters and bishops, while the local pagans, including the physicians, fled to the countryside in self-preservation. So even though the population was dwindling and fright seized the people, the church received a surge of growth.

Cyprian's remaining years saw more controversies and struggles. Following the course of the apostle Paul's ministry, there were no quiet years for Cyprian, just a constant barrage of trials, both internal in the church and external from the culture. During the mid-250s, Cyprian would engage in a lengthy polemic against the church at Rome over the issue of baptism; again, a subject of our next chapter. He exercised the strength of his pen, starting a letter-writing campaign against Stephen, the bishop of Rome, asserting his belief that baptism belonged to the true church and could only be administered by a valid representative of the church. When Stephen died and Sixtus II took Rome's *cathedra*, there was a brief time of respite, but it would not last long. Towards the end of the decade, the fires of persecution that had died down were rekindled.

Sentence and death

Emperor Valerian (253-260) came to power two years after Decius was killed at the Battle of Abitrus, during which time two others would rule in Rome. Valerian's attention was mostly on the northern and eastern regions of the empire where Goths and Burgundians threatened Thrace, Thessalonica, Nicea, and Nicomedia, wreaking havoc in major cities and torching the ones they could.[80] The greatest threat came from the Sasanians of Persia where Shapur I advanced his troops in from the east like a lance in the side of Rome, causing the empire to bleed significantly. Shapur I boasted that he had taken thirty-seven cities, a claim that does not seem exaggerated, but would withdraw

---

80 For a brief introduction to Valerian, see Michael Grant, *The Roman Emperors: A Biographical Guide to the Rulers of Imperial Rome 31 B.C. – A.D. 476* (New York: Barnes & Noble, 1985), pp. 163-68.

after pillaging the cities' goods, since expansion was not his goal. Valerian fell into the hands of the Persians in 260, who flayed him alive and then put his corpse on display.[81] Michael Grant explains the magnitude of an emperor of Rome falling into the hands of an enemy, saying that 'the capture of an emperor by a foreign foe was an unparalleled catastrophe, the nadir of Roman disgrace'.[82]

Valerian inherited an empire that was in dire straits. It is helpful to remember that Romans were experiencing the decimation of the plague at the same time their frontiers were being challenged. In an attempt to restore a semblance of order, Valerian issued an order that targeted higher-level officers in the church. These captains of the church could continue their worship of Jesus Christ, so long as they were also willing to offer sacrifice to the traditional gods.[83] Surely, he reasoned, these catastrophes that beset the empire would subside if the favor of the gods returned. He correlated the rapid growth of Christianity with the rapid decline of the empire, and sought to stem the tide of destruction that had knocked the entire empire off its path of domination and prosperity.

Cyprian was caught in the crosshairs of this persecution, along with Sixtus II of Rome, who was put to the sword early in the persecution. At first Cyprian was exiled from Carthage to Curubis for a period before he was brought back and confined to his home. During his banishment he had a vision that a trial was

---

81 See Frend, *The Rise of Christianity*, p. 308.

82 Michael Grant, *The Roman Emperors*, p. 165. Edward Gibbon cites a tradition that 'when Valerian sank under the weight of shame and grief, his skin, stuffed by straw, and formed into the likeness of a human figure, was preserved for ages in the most celebrated temple in Persia' (Grant, *The Roman Emperors*, p. 165).

83 See Cyprian, *Letter* 81.1. Cyprian writes, 'But the truth concerning them is as follows, that Valerian had sent a rescript to the Senate, to the effect that bishops and presbyters and deacons should immediately be punished; but that senators, and men of importance, and Roman knights, should lose their dignity, and moreover be deprived of their property; and if, when their means were taken away, they should persist in being Christians, then they should also lose their heads.'

coming where he would be sentenced to death. He envisioned the entire event before it played out in reality a year to the day of his martyrdom.[84] Many of his former friends, 'people of most illustrious rank and family, and noble with the world's distinctions', begged him to withdraw again, offering places where he might return to hiding.[85] Cyprian refused to abandon the flock again; this time his people would be better served by his death.

Soldiers came and seized Cyprian from his garden and took him to an officer's house where he would wait for his execution the next day.[86] Pontius, with a sense of awe, records Cyprian's demeanor as 'manifesting cheerfulness in his look and courage in his heart'.[87] Rumors quickly spread that the great bishop was detained and would be put to death in the morning and a large crowd gathered at the door of the officer's house to keep vigil, lest anything happen that night without their knowledge.

The trial itself was short and simple. Cyprian was arraigned before Galerius Maximus, the proconsul in Carthage, and was asked if he would sacrifice, and, of course, he would not. The proceedings from court that day were as follows:

> Maximus: You are Thascius Cyprianus?
> Cyprian: I am.
> Maximus: You put yourself forward as leader for these men of sacrilegious mind?
> Cyprian: Yes.
> Maxmimus: The most sacred emperors order you to perform the requisite ceremonies.
> Cyprian: I will not do it.
> Maximus: Consult your best interests.
> Cyprian: Do what you are ordered to do.

---

84 Pontius, *The Life and Passion of Cyprian* 12–13.

85 Pontius, *The Life and Passion of Cyprian* 14.

86 Cyprian spoke fondly of his gardens in his autobiographical letter *To Donatus* 1. Though he sold his property at his conversion, Pontius notes that God restored them to him as an act of mercy.

87 Pontius, *The Life and Passion of Cyprian* 15.

He was sentenced immediately to death, and many of his followers were so moved that they asked to be executed alongside him, though their petition was not granted.[88] The persecution was not meant to strike at every Christian, but was designed to decapitate the head of the church so that the body would die.

On the day of his passion, the clouds scattered leaving a canopy of blue skies and a warm sun. So many people came out that Pontius described them as a 'numberless army . . . as if they had come with an assembled troop to assault death itself'.[89] At the place of execution, the judge read his sentence from a tablet, the sentence which to Roman ears was worthy of death, but a sentence that was glorious to a Christian, namely that Cyprian was 'a standard-bearer of the sect, and an enemy of the gods, and one who was to be an example to his people'.[90] Cyprian would have nodded in humble agreement, proud that the Romans understood that he was a leader of the Christians, that he was an enemy of their gods, and that he was an example to his people.

The spot of his execution was level ground and was surrounded by trees. Because the crowd was thick, many people had to climb the trees and sit on branches to catch a glimpse.[91] The soldier assigned to be his executioner was almost unable to wield the sword having a 'failing right hand with trembling fingers', but he was ultimately able to carry out his task and execute Cyprian.[92] The date was 14 September 258. The crown of martyrdom, about which Cyprian spent a great deal of time writing, was now his.[93]

Several of the faithful gathered at the execution spread napkins and clothes to soak up some of the blood for later veneration,

---

88 Sage, *Cyprian*, p. 351.

89 Pontius, *The Life and Passion of Cyprian* 16.

90 Pontius, *The Life and Passion of Cyprian* 17.

91 Pontius, *The Life and Passion of Cyprian* 18. Pontius makes the parallel to Zaccheus.

92 Pontius, *The Life and Passion of Cyprian* 18.

93 See Cyprian's use of this verse with martyrdom, in *On the Lapsed* 18.

an early example of relics. His body was buried that day, but exhumed at night to protect it from pagans who might dig him up out of curiosity, and he was reburied somewhere off the street of Mappaliensis near the fish ponds.[94] The bishop who had helped guide the church during a turbulent decade, in both the life of the church and secular society, was dead, but his influence remained very much alive. As far as the Roman authorities were concerned, they had achieved what they wanted—they had silenced the tongue of a dangerous revolutionary. As is often the case, the opposite proved true. Søren Kierkegaard would rightly say many centuries later, 'The tyrant dies and his rule is over, the martyr dies and his rule begins.'[95] This proved quite true for Valerian and Cyprian; the martyr overshadowed the tyrant. Valerian died several years later and history barely remembers him. Cyprian's death, however, brought a sense of immortality, amplifying his voice and achieving for him worldwide renown, even to our day.

Cyprian and Scripture

Before moving away from our biographical sketch of Cyprian, it is beneficial to examine Cyprian's writings and his use of Scripture. Michael Fahey, whose study of Cyprian's use of Scripture is exhaustive, comments, 'The clearest influence on Cyprian was Scripture itself. In this sense Cyprian was a man of a single book.'[96] Immediately upon his conversion, Cyprian

---

94 Sage, *Cyprian*, p. 352.

95 Søren Kierkegaard, *Papers and Journals: A Selection*, trans. Alistair Hannay (London: Penguin, 1996), p. 352. See also the fascinating article by Jack Mulder, Jr., 'Cyprian of Carthage: Kierkegaard, Cyprian, and the "urgent needs of the times,"' in *Kierkegaard and the Patristic and Medieval Traditions*, ed. Jon Stewart (Kierkegaard Research: Sources, Reception, and Resources, vol. 4; Burlington, VT: Ashgate, 1998), pp. 67-92. In an ironic way both Cyprian and Kierkegaard argued for rigorous Christian living—the former because of persecution; the latter because of the lack of persecution (67).

96 Michael Fahey, *Cyprian and the Bible: a Study in Third-Century Exegesis* (Tübingen: J. C. B. Mohr, 1971), p. 28. I am indebted to Michel Fahey's groundbreaking work in this section.

began to devour Scripture. He must have been a voracious reader with an eidetic memory, because in a short period of time he demonstrated a command over Scripture, citing passages from all across the canon.[97] Having grown up in a pagan family and in secular culture, his exposure to the Bible would have been minimal or non-existent before he became a Christian.

In his writings, Cyprian was intentional in his use of Scripture—the Bible alone was authoritative for truth. He opens his *Exhortation to Martyrdom, To Fortunatus*, saying, 'For it is little to arouse God's people by the trumpet call of our voice, unless we confirm the faith of believers, and their valour dedicated and devoted to God, by the *divine readings*.'[98] His voice, however eloquent, could not awaken people to action unless his ideas were thoroughly soaked in the divine readings, that is, Scripture. Again, he wanted to make clear to Fortunatus that his thoughts came from the Bible and not his own wisdom, because Scripture has authority. He writes, 'I might subjoin sections of the Lord's word, and establish what I had proposed by the authority of the divine teaching.'[99]

Cyprian possessed a 'reverence for the Word of God',[100] believing that Scripture is inspired. Returning to his treatise, *Exhortation to Martyrdom*, Cyprian says that he is 'instructed by the aid of divine inspiration'.[101] Although he uses the word

---

97 Phillip Campbell has a thorough breakdown of Cyprian's use of Scripture in his appendix to Cyprian's collected writings. Cyprian cites the Bible 1,490 times. To give just a taste of Cyprian's use of the Bible, he cited Matthew most frequently (175 citations), then Psalms (127), John (121), Isaiah (109), and 1 Corinthians (80). See Campbell, *The Complete Works of Saint Cyprian of Carthage*, pp. 555-62. See Fahey for a similar table, *Cyprian and the Bible*, pp. 42-43. There figures do not line up exactly but this is because allusions are counted and these are far more subjective. But this gives a general impression of Cyprian's use of the Bible. Also, see Fahey for a good discussion of Cyprian's canon, *Cyprian and the Bible*, pp. 40-43.

98 Cyprian, *Exhortation to Martyrdom, To Fortunatus* 1, emphasis added.

99 Cyprian, *Exhortation to Martyrdom, To Fortunatus* 3. At the start of *On Mortality*, Cyprian states the entire treatise is a 'discourse based on Holy Scripture'.

100 Michael Fahey, *Cyprian and the Bible*, p. 29.

101 Cyprian, *Exhortation to Martyrdom, To Fortunatus* 1.

'inspiration' only three times, Cyprian uses several other phrases that confirm his belief that God is the author of Scripture, commenting for instance on Deuteronomy 24:26: 'since we know, according to the faith of the divine Scriptures, [that] God Himself [is] their author'.[102] Because the Bible is of divine origin, 'Cyprian hardly ever uses a Scriptural citation without identifying the text as biblical, by means of an introductory formula,' which was typically, *scriptum est*, or 'it is written'.[103] This formula is extended to the Apocrypha as well, from which Cyprian freely cites with equal authority as Scripture, at times introducing a quote by saying, 'As it says in Scripture'.[104] No doubt that Cyprian, along with most Fathers in the early church, valued the Apocrypha highly.

Cyprian's use of Scripture is straightforward, lacking the frills and innovations of some of his contemporaries.[105] He is not, for instance, frequently given to the questionable allegory of his contemporary Origen. To be sure, allegory was not foreign to Cyprian's hermeneutic, especially in his interpretation of the Song of Songs, though allegorical interpretation of this book

---

102 Cyprian, *Letter* 51.27.

103 Michael Fahey, *Cyprian and the Bible*, p. 29.

104 Approximately 12 percent of Cyprian's scriptural citations come from Apocrypha. Primarily, Cyprian cites Sirach (34 times), Wisdom (18), and Tobit (14). See Campbell, *The Complete Works of Saint Cyprian of Carthage*, pp. 558, 560. According to the forthcoming Gallagher-Meade hypothesis of canon formation in the early church (Edmon L Gallagher and John D. Meade, *The Biblical Canon Lists from Early Christianity: Texts and Analysis* [Oxford: Oxford University Press, 2017]), we cannot conclude that just because Cyprian quoted the Apocrypha as Scripture (or that he used introductory phrases such as 'it is written' to introduce these texts) that he considered these works as canon. Gallagher and Meade discovered that certain Fathers have a delineated canon list that excludes the Apocrypha and yet the Father will still cite the work as Scripture. Therefore, Scripture does not equal canon. Without a canonical list, we can only observe how Cyprian uses texts; we cannot assert that he elevated the Apocrypha to the level of canon.

105 As influential as Cyprian was, he does not even warrant an essay in the comprehensive work *Dictionary of Major Biblical Interpreters*, ed. Donald K. McKim (Downers Grove: IVP Academic, 2007). This owes to the fact that he was not creative in his approach to Scripture.

was standard. When it came to his writings on the church, Cyprian used all sorts of figural readings to argue that the church must remain united. Given his penchant for addressing moral concerns as they arose, Cyprian normally shied away from historical passages and the like, and opted instead to focus on clear-cut passages that spoke to behavior. On this point Nienke Vos has observed: 'the fact that moral categories are dominant in the bishop's understanding of Scripture explains why other biblical material, such as miracle stories, historical passages and parables, [do] not figure so prominently in his oeuvre.'[106] Parables, miracles, and historical accounts are not useful weapons in his arsenal that is stocked for virtue. Cyprian wanted to press his reader into submission to the sacred text. For Cyprian, 'the Bible [is] a collection of divine sayings and commands requiring obedience'.[107] Scripture transformed Cyprian's own thoughts and served as the basis for all of his own contributions.

Cyprian the writer

Latin Christianity took off at the turn of the third century in North Africa. Before this even the church in Rome spoke Greek. It was not until Tertullian that Latin theology began and would eventually become the language of the church. From Africa's northern shore came some of Christianity's best minds, the likes of Tertullian, Augustine, and between them, Cyprian. While Augustine is by all accounts the most gifted Latin-speaking theologian in the history of the Patristic era, Tertullian is also widely regarded as one of the greatest thinkers in that era.

---

106 Nienke Vos, 'Cyprian's Use of Scripture in Letter 58,' in *Cyprian of Carthage: Studies in His Life, Language, and Thought*, ed. Henk Bakker, Paul van Geest, and Hans van Loon (Leuven: Peeters, 2010), p. 67. Vos is working off of Fahey's work on this point (Fahey, *Cyprian and the Bible*, p. 40).

107 Michael Fahey, *Cyprian and the Bible*, p. 40.

Cyprian, though, has been chided by some who consider his work 'untheological'[108] or lacking in 'speculative theology'.[109]

The ancients did not agree with this assessment of Cyprian made by modern scholars. Jerome summarized the early church's opinion about Cyprian's writings: 'It is superfluous to weave together the sign of his genius, since his works are brighter than the sun.'[110] Gregory Nanzianzus, speaking earlier than Jerome, said about Cyprian's writings, 'The many brilliant works that he authored for us stand as testament to his erudition, for thanks to the loving-kindness of God, who makes all things and changes them, he put his education to better use and made unreason bow to reason.'[111] Had Cyprian remained unconverted, teaching rhetoric or practicing law, his name would more than likely escape us today. Instead, he put his intellect to work, crafting a handful of treatises and dozens of letters that would cement his place in history. That last bit of Gregory's comment, about making unreason bow to reason, showcased Cyprian's rigorous logic that he set to the tune of brilliant rhetoric.

When Cyprian's training and education as an orator were lit by the Holy Spirit, he became a powerful communicator of God's Word. In many ways his life mirrors that of Augustine, who was born just shy of one hundred years after Cyprian's martyrdom. As noted above, their conversions took a similar path and they were both gifted with superior abilities, not to mention their

---

108 Paul Parvis, 'The Teaching of the Fathers: Cyprian and the Hours of Prayer,' *Clergy* 69 (1984): p. 206.

109 Ronald E. Heine, 'Cyprian and Novation,' in *The Cambridge History of Early Christian Literature*, ed. Frances Young, Lewis Ayres, and Andrew Louth (Cambridge: Cambridge University Press, 2004), p. 156. For these citations on the perception of Cyprian as one lacking in theological acumen, see David J. Downs, 'Prosopological Exegesis in Cyprian's *De opera et eleemosynis*,' *Journal of Theological Interpretation* 6.2 (2012): p. 280.

110 Jerome, *On Illustrious Men* 67. It should be apparent that Jerome thought highly of Cyprian. For Jerome's affinity to Cyprian, see Simone Deléani, 'Présence de Cyprien dans les oeuvres de Jérôme sur la virginité,' in *Jérôme entre l'occident et l'orient*, ed. Yves-Marie Duval (Paris: Études Augustiniennes, 1988), pp. 61-82.

111 Gregory Nanzianzus, *Orations* 24.7, trans. Martha Vinson, p. 145.

exposure to classical works of literature. Augustine liked to speak of using the wisdom of the world in the employ of the church as plundering the Egyptians. Cyprian, Augustine suggests, was a master at this. 'Do we not see with what a quantity of gold and silver and garments Cyprian, that most persuasive teacher and most blessed martyr, was loaded when he came out of Egypt?'[112] When Cyprian emerged out of his pagan life, he plundered the best that the world had to offer and translated it in ways that would be helpful for the church. His works may be bereft of mention to the body of classical works that preceded him, but his power of persuasion came from emulating the works of the classical giants.

In addition to his insatiable desire to drink from the well of Scripture, Cyprian was also an avid learner of theology. Jerome records that Cyprian would daily call for 'the Master', by whom he meant Tertullian, though surprisingly, he never mentions Tertullian.[113] It may well be that Cyprian does not cite Tertullian because of Tertullian's foray into Montanism late in life—he likely wanted to distance himself from any suspicion of Montanism. Yet some of Cyprian's writings are nearly identical to those of Tertullian, such as *On the Dress of Virgins*. Had Jerome never told us that Cyprian routinely asked for Tertullian's works, it would still be readily apparent that Cyprian was indebted to his forebear, whose influence can be detected on nearly every page. John Faulkner said it best, 'Cyprian fed his soul on [Tertullian].'[114]

As a writer, Cyprian can remind one of Luther who said that he wrote and preached best when he was angry.[115] The tone of

---

112 Augustine, *One Christian Doctrine* 2.40.

113 Michael Fahey calls Jerome's comment 'largely exaggerated' (*Cyprian and the Bible*, 27), though Cyprian's dependence on Tertullian seems undeniable.

114 John Faulkner, *Cyprian: the Churchman*, 14.

115 To quote Luther, 'I have no better remedy than anger. If I want to write, pray, preach well, then I must be angry. Then my entire blood supply refreshes itself, my mind is made keen and all temptations depart' (see *What Luther Says: An Anthology*, vol. 1, compiled by Ewald M. Plass [St. Louis: Concordia Publishing, 1959], 74.27).

Cyprian's writings is sharp, the rhetoric punchy, and often there is more than a hint of sarcasm.[116] One can almost imagine the redness of face and the tight grip of his pen as he sat down to write a scathing letter to Stephen of Rome, or the squint of his eyes and the furrow of his brow as he wrote against the followers of Novatian. There is no mistaking his passion. Others must agree or repent—there was no middle ground, unless of course, it was the middle ground he advocated. In this case, the other positions were extremes to be avoided. This makes him entertaining to read, again reminiscent of his predecessor Tertullian.

Cyprian wrote treatises on the church, polemical pieces ranging from disputations against the Jews to an apologetic, tracts on spiritual formation, and a corpus of letters covering a vast array of topics. His major works were *On the Unity of the Church*, arguing that unity is integral to the nature of the church, and *On the Lapsed*, discussing what should be done with those who buckled when asked to sacrifice. His only apology to the state was when he wrote *An Address to Demetrianus* in which he lambasted the Proconsul for his participation in the persecution. In response to the prospect of martyrdom, Cyprian wrote *On Mortality* and *Exhortation to Martyrdom*, encouraging believers to endure during persecution, so that they might gain the crown of life. Following in the vein of Tertullian, Cyprian also composed numerous ethical treatises like *On the Dress of Virgins*, *On the Vanity of Idols*, *On Works and Alms*, *On the Advantage of Patience*, and *On Jealousy and Envy*. Regrettably, the one thing we are missing from him is his sermons.[117] Given Cyprian's influence in his own day, and his

---

116 I disagree with Lactantius and Jerome who described Cyprian's writings as a transparent and tranquil stream (Lactantius, *Divine Institutes* 1.25 and Jerome, *Epistles* 58.10). See Ryan Grant, *The Complete Works of Saint Cyprian of Carthage*, xii. Faulkner was more on the mark when he said, 'Cyprian was a dealer in sarcasm' (*Cyprian: the Churchman*, 106). Sarcasm was an important tool in ancient rhetoric.

117 *Pace* Adolf von Harnack who believed that a snippet of one of Cyprian's sermons may be found embedded in Pontius's *The Life and Passion of Cyprian* in 3:6-10 (See Adolf von Harnack, *Das Leben Cyprians von Pontius: die erste christliche Biographie* [Leipzig: J. C. Hinrichs'sche Buchhandlung, 1913], p. 10). Even if von Harnack is

artistic flare in the writings we do have, we can assume that his sermons were nothing short of spectacular.

Cyprian's most enduring legacy is his work on the church. Each controversy he found himself in could be reduced to this question—what is the nature of the church? The specific questions he addressed were varied. Can the church be divided or should the church be like the seamless garment that covered the body of Christ? Who has the ultimate authority in the church? What was meant by Jesus' installation of Peter as the rock upon which the church would be built: does this refer to one pontiff or does each bishop have equal claim as an heir of Peter? How should the sacraments function and how should they be given? Could the immorality or unorthodoxy of the person administering baptism nullify the legitimacy of the sacrament? Cyprian was the first writer in the church to give serious thought to these questions, and because of this, he has solidified his place in the history of the church.

One cannot help but wonder what might have attracted Cyprian's pen had not the pressing issues of his day forced his hand. Would he have helped prepare the way for the Trinitarian controversies of the next century? Would he have written a practical work on pastoring? There is no way to know. However, in the providence of God, Cyprian did feel compelled to respond to the demands of his day and, because he did, he developed an ecclesiology that would guide the church to the eve of the

correct, we are still missing what must have been hundreds of sermons preached over the course of his tenure as bishop. See also Charles Bobertz, 'An Analysis of Vita Cypriani 3.6-10 and the Attribution of *Ad Quirinum* to Cyprian of Carthage,' *Vigiliae Christianae* 46 (1992): pp. 112-28 for an analysis of this section of Pontius's work, though Bobertz's intent is to show that Cyprian did not compose *Ad Quirinum*. Peter Sanlon, who has contributed a tremendous work on Augustine's rhetoric, argues that many of Cyprian's writings have a sermonic feel, though we should not press this too far. Most of Cyprian's writings were occasional, written to particular audiences for particular reasons. See Peter Sanlon, *Augustine's Theology of Preaching* (Minneapolis: Fortress, 2014), pp. 10-11. The closest example of this could be Cyprian's *On Patience* which begins, 'As I am about to speak, beloved brethren,' which opens as a sermon might. C. F. A. Borchardt asserts too confidently, '[*On Patience*] is obvious that it was initially a sermon' ('Cyprian on Patience,' *St. Hist. Eccl. XVIII* 2 [1992]: 19). We are left to speculate about Cyprian's preaching.

Reformation, and the Roman Catholic Church into the present day. It is to the controversies that drew his attention that now draw ours.

2

CYPRIAN AND HIS CONTROVERSIES

The year before Cyprian became bishop of Carthage (c. A.D. 248) Rome celebrated her millennial birthday.[1] No expense was spared for the festivities, as coins from this time show that lions, deer, and hippopotami were brought into the Circus Maximus for the amusement of the people, along with the deaths of more than a thousand gladiators. The Secular Games (*Ludi Saeculares*), as they were called, were celebrated every hundred years, but were of particular importance in A.D. 248 because Rome had turned a thousand years old. The games were partially an attempt to distract the people from the crises that were dogging the Empire. Enemies of Rome were poised for attack, the economy teetered on the brink of collapse, and soon the emperorship would change hands again.

Philip I (r. A.D. 244-9), known as Philip the Arab, was Caesar during this time and was responsible for staging the games. Like other emperors of the third century, Philip had to take his troops to the frontier to fight Germanic tribes that had crossed the Danube, taking the title 'Germanicus Maximus' for himself. While he was handling affairs in the north, trouble broke out within the ranks in the eastern provinces as two other men vied for the throne. Fearing usurpation that would sunder the Empire, Philip volunteered before the Senate to abdicate, though the city

---

1 The year A.D. 247 is according to the Gregorian calendar designed around the Christian faith centuries later. For the Romans, the year A.D. 247 was the year 1,000 AUC (*ab urbe condita*), or 'from the founding of the city.'

prefect, Decius, said that such a move was unnecessary. Decius remarked that these men were unpopular with the troops and they would soon be assassinated, and he proved right. Because of Decius's political savvy the troops began to support him and hail him as emperor, even to his repeated protest. Philip did not believe Decius's modesty and marched against him, and although numbers were on his side, he was easily defeated and committed suicide at Verona.[2] Ironically, by setting out against Decius, Philip brought about his own demise and Decius's rise to power.

Eusebius actually suggests that Philip was the first Christian emperor, claiming, 'Word has it that [Philip] was a Christian and wanted to join with believers in the prayers of the church on the day of the last Easter vigil,'[3] and that Decius picked up the sword against Christians 'because of his hostility to Philip.'[4] Besides the peace the church enjoyed during Philip's reign, nothing else corroborates Eusebius's testimony and so it should not be given much weight.[5] The far more likely reason why Decius started to persecute the church is that he genuinely wanted to restore the Empire to her former glory.

By the time that Decius became emperor in 249, the games were already fading into memory. What should have inspired hope and unity among the people were just an elaborate façade that failed to recapture the *esprit de corps* that had slipped away

---

2   Frend, *The Rise of Christianity* (Philadelphia: Fortress Press, 1984), p. 319.

3   Eusebius, *Church History* 6.34, trans. Paul L. Maier (Grand Rapids: Kregel, 1999), p. 231.

4   Eusebius, *Church History* 6.39, trans. Paul L. Maier, 233.

5   See Warwick Bell, *Rome in the East: The Transformation of an Empire*, 2nd ed. (London and New York: Routledge, 2016), p.470, who says 'Modern scholarship has ranged from complete rejection to complete affirmation, with most taking the middle road, conceding that Philip at least "dabbled" in Christianity.' Yasmine Zahran suggests the reason for the uncertainty is the private nature of Philip's faith. She writes, 'Philip was emperor of all, and Christian to himself. It is hardly surprising that the pagan authors are silent on the subject of his Christianity—there was nothing to comment on' (*Philip the Arab: A Study in Prejudice* [London: Stacey International], p. 113).

over the past few decades. Decius was smart enough to know that drastic measures were needed in order to stabilize the Empire and set a new trajectory. Faced with peril on every side, the Empire desperately needed the favor of the gods. The questions were these: (1) why were the gods visiting misfortune on the Empire, and (2) how could their blessings return? For Decius the answer was that many had forsaken the worship of Roman deities and the solution was to start a revival of religion.

Decius took the unprecedented step of issuing an empire-wide edict that called for universal sacrifice, accompanied by the threat of punishment for those who refused. Bryan Litfin notes, 'No longer would enforcement be reactionary; persecution now came from the top as part of an empire-wide program.'[6] Decius exerted his power as the *pontifex maximus*, the chief priest as it were, of the Roman cult.[7] Just months after becoming emperor, on January 3, 250, Decius issued an edict that every citizen would have to offer a sacrifice to the gods, pour out a libation, and/or burn incense to the emperor's *genius*. Failure to obtain a certificate proving one's compliance to the emperor's order would result in a fine, exile, imprisonment, torture, or death.

Persecution in the Early Church

Before moving forward in our discussion of the Decian persecution and the repercussions it had in Cyprian's ministry, a brief excursus is helpful to understand the nature and extent of persecution in the early centuries. Litfin describes modern misconception about persecution in the early church, saying, 'A lot of nonsense is tossed around in the popular media about

---

6   Bryan Litfin, *Early Christian Martyr Stories: An Evangelical Introduction with New Translations* (Grand Rapids: Baker Academic, 2014), p. 5.

7   Allen Brent, *Cyprian and Roman Carthage* (Cambridge: Cambridge University Press, 2010), p. 117. Since Augustus, the role of *pontifex maximus* was taken over by the emperor. This term was later taken up by the bishop of Rome to demonstrate his primacy as the head bishop, though interestingly, Tertullian first applied this to the Roman bishop Callixtus in jest (*On Modesty* 1).

the ancient church.'[8] In the modern imagination, Christians were herded into the Colosseum by the thousands, or tens of thousands, where they had their fleshed ripped off by hungry beasts or were run through by muscular gladiators. While this did happen periodically, there was no effort to exterminate Christianity wholesale, at least not until the end of the third century. Prior to Decius's edict, and then Diocletian's systemic persecution (c. 303) called the 'Great Persecution,' the church was harassed sporadically and locally.

Martyrdom, however, is critical to the foundation of the Christian faith. That is to say, the Christian faith was established in martyrdom and has a heritage of flourishing through suffering. Jesus of Nazareth was mocked, whipped, pierced, and crucified for His belief that He was the Son of God and His followers received the same maltreatment, thereby proving Jesus' words that 'a servant is not greater than his master. If they persecuted me, they will also persecute you' (John 15:20). By the time John wrote this most, if not all, the disciples had experienced the truth of these words firsthand. Tradition tells us that all of the apostles were martyred, excluding Judas's suicide and John's exile. Peter was crucified upside down, Paul was beheaded,[9] James was tossed from the parapet of the Temple, and when this failed to kill him, he was stoned and then clubbed to death.[10] All of the others faced a similar fate, as did many Christians in the early centuries. Christianity is a religion of martyrdom.

Not only is Christianity historically persecuted, but the early church believed that persecution is what made the faith sparkle, as if martyrdom is the crown jewel of spirituality. Christians suffered with grace and love, which is what made Christianity distinctive and even desirable to the pagan world. Ignatius said

---

8   Litfin, *Early Christian Martyr Stories*, 2.

9   For the tradition of Peter and Paul's death given here, see Tertullian, *Prescription against Heretics* 36.

10 See Eusebius, *Church History*, 2.23, trans. Paul L. Maier, 81–83.

on the road to his execution, 'Christianity is greatest when it is hated by the world.'[11] Tertullian observed perhaps the first church growth strategy when he said, 'The blood of the martyrs is the seed [of the church].'[12] Both Ignatius and Tertullian recognized the undeniable power of the martyred life. Persecution, which sought to stop the spread of Christianity, had a paradoxical effect that served to grow the faith. Blood truly was the seed that grew the early church.

The first account of persecution in Africa came in the account of the *Scillitan Martyrs* (c. A.D. 180), which we briefly discussed last chapter. Even our knowledge of this event is limited, since there is only a short account of the trial. Saturninus the proconsul arraigned Speratus, Nartzalus, Cittinus, Donata, Vestia, Secunda, and others (*et ceteros ritu Christiano*) and charged them with failure to honor the emperor. The trial was not a witch hunt. Saturninus gave the Christians ample opportunity to recant and burn incense in honor of the emperor, professing their allegiance to the Roman state. To him, Christians had abandoned sound thinking but could be restored to good standing with a simple offering. The Christians refused, but Saturninus was still willing to grant a thirty-day reprieve for the Christians to think it over. They turned down his offer because there was nothing to reconsider, and so they were condemned to the sword. They reacted to their sentence with the humble reply, *Deo gratias agimus*—'we give thanks to God.'[13] The narrator ends the account with reference to their martyrs' crowns and their eternal reign with the Triune God.

---

11 See Ignatius, 'The Letter of Ignatius to the Romans,' 3.3, in *The Apostolic Fathers*, ed. and trans. Michael W. Holmes, 3rd ed. (Grand Rapids: Baker Academic, 2007), p. 229.

12 Tertullian, *Apology* 50. This is the common paraphrase used, but the text actually reads, 'Nor does your cruelty, however exquisite, avail you; it is rather a temptation to us. The oftener we are mown down by you, the more in number we grow; the blood of Christians is seed.'

13 *The Passion of S. Perpetua*, ed. J. Armitage Robinson, *Texts and Studies* 1.2 (Eugene, O.R.: Wipf and Stock, n.d.), p. 116. This contains the account of the Scillitan Martyrs as well.

Two decades later another martyrdom occurred, this time in Cyprian's hometown of Carthage (c. A.D. 202).[14] Cyprian was probably just a toddler when Perpetua and her female servant Felicity awaited their execution. A small band of Christians were condemned because they refused to deny Christ. Saturus became fodder for leopards, while Perpetua was tied to a vicious cow that slung her about, but when this failed to kill her, she was run through with a sword at the hand of a novice (*tirunculus*), who struck several blows before Perpetua put the blade to her own neck.

Several aspects of the story stand out for their heinousness. First, among the handful of men that were killed, there were two women also martyred, and not just any women, but Perpetua who was of noble blood. To add yet another layer of astonishment, Perpetua had a nursing infant at her breast. The story highlights the monstrous lengths the Romans were willing to go to in order to squelch a peaceful religion. More than that, these accounts were meant to inspire other Christians about the glory that awaited the martyred. One danger, then, was that Christians would begin to pursue martyrdom.

The best example of the latter is Origen in the city of Alexandria in Egypt. Eusebius tells the story that when Septimius Severus (r. A.D. 193–211) was emperor, Origen's father, Leonides, was arrested and beheaded. Origen desired to be like his father and he yearned for martyrdom, even as a youth of seventeen. His mother, however, had a clever way of stopping her son.

> Such a passion for martyrdom possessed Origen, boy though he was, that he wanted to court danger and plunge into the conflict. In fact, he came within a hair's breadth of ending his days, had not divine providence acted through his mother for the good of humankind. First she tried words, pleading with

---

14 Many scholars believe that Tertullian authored Perpetua's martyrdom account, which is likely given that he was the most recognizable Christian in Carthage at the turn of the third century.

him to spare a mother's feelings, but when he learned that his father had been thrown into prison, he was filled with a craving for martyrdom. Seeing that he was more determined than ever, she hid all his clothes and so forced him to stay at home.[15]

To obtain martyrdom, Origen would have to seek danger in the nude! Apparently this whimsical move cooled the passion that was about to boil over in Origen. Not everyone had a mother who was willing or cunning enough to hide their clothes. Many sought martyrdom and were granted their wish. Scholars have used terms like 'voluntary martyrdom' or 'provoked martyrdom' to express this phenomenon in early Christianity.[16] Equally, and unsurprisingly, there were those who wished to avoid martyrdom at any price. We meet both in the course of Cyprian's writings.

While we must be careful not to over-exaggerate martyrdom in the early church, we must also avoid recent attempts to expunge large portions of persecution and martyrdom from ancient history. The most current form of this argument comes from Candida Moss in her academic book *Ancient Christian Martyrdom: Diverse Practices, Theologies, and Traditions* which was also distilled for popular audiences under the title *The Myth of Persecution: How Early Christians Invented a Story of Martyrdom*.[17] As already noted, we can dispense with the notion that Romans practiced open season on Christians for three hundred years. Persecution came at sporadic times and seldom stretched the expanse of the Empire. Usually it was local and circumstantial, and there is evidence that the Empire would try to avoid persecution if at all possible.[18] However, to deny or devalue the

---

15   Eusebius, *Church History* 6.2, trans. Paul Maier, 207-08.

16   See Candida Moss, *Ancient Christian Martyrdom: Diverse Practices, Theologies, and Traditions* (New Haven: Yale University Press, 2012), pp. 149-55.

17   See Candida Moss, *The Myth of Persecution: How Early Christians Invented a Story of Martyrdom* (New York: HarperOne, 2013).

18   In one of the most famous letters of antiquity, Pliny the Younger sent a letter to Emperor Trajan asking his advice on how to handle Christianity (*Letter* 10.96). Trajan's response is cautious (*Letter* 10.97). He instructs his governor not to seek

reality of persecution is just as irresponsible and neglectful of the evidence.

According to Moss, 'Very few Christians died, and when they did, they were often executed for what we in the modern world would call political reasons. There is a difference between persecution and prosecution.'[19] While she acknowledges that one cannot neatly separate politics and religion, especially in the ancient world where every aspect of life was infused with religion, Moss nevertheless pushes persecution to the side.[20] The problem with moving the reality of persecution to the periphery is that Christians were prosecuted because they would not sacrifice to the gods or burn incense to the emperor on the basis of their belief that God alone is to be worshipped. How is this not the persecution of which Jesus spoke when He promised His followers 'they will lay their hands on you and persecute you, delivering you up to the synagogues and prisons, and you will be brought before kings and governors for my name's sake. This will be your opportunity to bear witness'? (Luke 21:12-13). It is significant that Jesus used the word *martyrion* in v. 13. This word originally meant to bear witness at a trial, but soon took on the meaning of witnessing for one's faith unto death. In essence, Jesus promises that His followers would be prosecuted in Jewish synagogues and in secular courts, and that it might cost them their lives.

Persecution and prosecution were the same thing in these cases. Being prosecuted for disobeying laws that violate religious

---

out Christians, but that if any should be found, they are to be punished.

19 Moss, *The Myth of Persecution*, 14.

20 More than anything else, Moss reacts against modern Christians using the narrative of persecution to describe the current political landscape (*The Myth of Persecution*, 8-13). Granted, many Christians have a tendency to overuse the word martyrdom, and shamefully this is done for political gain at times. But to lessen the sacrifice of those who gave their lives because they would not allow the state to infringe on their beliefs is a travesty. The story of persecution in the early church is desperately needed for those in our day who are being called upon to lay down their lives for the name of Christ.

conviction is germane to persecution. We empty persecution of its meaning if it does not include prosecution for refusal to do something that would violate a person's faith. Moss does not see it this way. She writes, 'There is something different about being prosecuted under a law—however unjust—that is not designed to target or rout out any particular group. It may be unfortunate, it may be unfair, but it is not persecution.'[21]

Thus, if we return to the Decian persecution, Moss claims, 'Even the so-called Decian persecution in 250 C.E. was about political uniformity, not religious persecution. Nothing in our evidence for Decius's legislation mentions targeting Christians.'[22] At one point she recognizes that 'the decree required that Christians apostatize or die' but still believes that Decius's edict did not constitute persecution against Christians.[23] In response it is important to acknowledge that just because Christians were not targeted for being Christians, does not mean that this was not a legitimate persecution against them. They may not have been sought out for being Christians, but they were killed for being Christians just the same. To quote Moss once more, 'If we are going to condemn the Romans for persecuting the Christians, then surely they need to have done it deliberately or at least have been *aware* they were doing it.'[24] If Moss is correct, then Jesus did not suffer persecution, even though he interpreted His own death in this way (again, see John 15:20). Wasn't Jesus just an insurrectionist in the eyes of Rome and prosecuted for His crime? We must dissent from Moss. Christians were persecuted

---

21 Moss, *The Myth of Persecution*, 14–15. I understand Moss's point and I believe her point is well-taken in certain instances. Take for instance Dietrich Bonhoeffer who was killed, not for his faith, but for his attempt to assassinate Hitler. Should he be considered a martyr? Perhaps not. But early Christians do not fit this category. They were killed because they were asked to do things that would have severed their souls from Christ for eternity.

22 Moss, *The Myth of Persecution*, 15.

23 Moss, *The Myth of Persecution*, 148.

24 Moss, *The Myth of Persecution*, 150.

for their faith, as their Lord had been, and they suffered greatly for His name in the mid third century.

Wilken observes how the various heads of the churches were severed at the onset of Decius's persecution. He writes, 'In the first month [after Decius's decree], Alexander, bishop of Jerusalem, was arrested and died in prison, Fabian, bishop of Antioch, was martyred, Dionysius, bishop of Alexandria, was apprehended and imprisoned . . . . Origen, the Church's most prominent thinker, living in Caesarea in Palestine, was cruelly tortured on the rack,'[25] Fabian the bishop of Rome died in prison, and Cyprian fled into self-imposed exile. Notable names from notable cities distributed across the Empire were tortured and killed. The Empire targeted church leaders, and by doing this, they unwittingly fulfilled Jesus' words, 'Strike the shepherd and the sheep of the flock will be scattered' (Matt 26:31). Though Jesus was applying these words to Himself, it held true for the early church when the shepherds of the flock, the bishops and presbyters, would be cut down, which caused many in the church to scatter out of fear. Even though the sword of persecution might not have touched as many heads as has been believed, it was the heads that it did touch that made such an impact on the early church.

The emperor's order must have been carried out swiftly since such a large number of Christian leaders were persecuted quickly after the edict was issued.[26] The edict is lost but examples of certificates (*libelli* [literally, 'little books'])do remain from those who did offer sacrifice. One well-known example comes from Egypt:

Libellus from a Village in Egypt, Dated Summer 250

---

25 Wilken, *The First Thousand Years*, 68. It is possible that Wilken missteps when he speaks of Fabian of Antioch. Probably he is thinking of Fabian of Rome and/or Babylas of Antioch (Frend, *The Rise of Christianity*, 319), though Babylas was killed near the end of the persecution in 253.

26 By January 20, Fabian was executed (Frend, *The Rise of Early Christianity*, 319).

[1st hand]. To those appointed to oversee the sacrifices. From Aurelia Charis of the village of Theadelphia. I have always been constant in sacrificing and shown piety to the gods, and not too, in your presence, in accordance with the order I have poured a libation, and I have offered sacrifice, and I have eaten of the sacrificial offerings. May you prosper.

[2nd hand]. We, Aurelius Serenus and Aurelius Hermus, saw you sacrificing.

[3rd hand]. I, Hermas, certify it.

[1st hand]. The year one of the Emperor Caesar Gaius Messius Quintus Traianus Decius Pius Felix Augustus, Pauni 22 [June 16, 250].[27]

It was standard for these certificates to indicate that the individual had *always* sacrificed to the gods. This unbroken allegiance to the gods was a way of underlining a person's patriotism and devotion to the emperor. The sacrifice would be witnessed and each certificate would be notarized. In Carthage there was a commission established of magistrates and five prominent citizens (*primores*) who oversaw the sacrifices to ensure that they were being performed.[28]

The result was widespread obeisance to the will of the emperor, even by many professing Christians who went at once to offer their sacrifices. Cyprian was appalled that so many rushed to sacrifice before their hand was even forced. He lamented, 'Ah misery! . . . They indeed did not wait to be apprehended ere they ascended, or to be interrogated ere they denied. Many were

---

27 Wilken, *The First Thousand Years*, 69. For an extended treatment on *libelli*, see J. R. Knipfing, 'The Libelli of the Decian Persecution,' *Harvard Theological Review* 16 (1923) pp. 345–90.

28 Frend, *The Rise of Early Christianity*, 320.

conquered before the battle, prostrated before the attack.'[29] The white flag of surrender was raised before threats were carried out. So many people flooded the place of sacrifice that the magistrates would have to turn them away when evening came.[30] Cyprian says that by scurrying off to sacrifice, they really were hastening their own death, even though they were trying to save their lives. Cyprian, of course, had in mind the judgment of God that was going to befall them due to their surrender of the faith. In God's economy whoever wishes to save this ephemeral life will lose the only life that counts (Mark 8:35).

In the midst of those who acquiesced under the threats, there were also stories of heroic Christians who were unwilling to sacrifice and paid dearly for their convictions. Celerinus, for instance, suffered so egregiously that the title martyr was bestowed on him while he was still living! He had been imprisoned in Rome where he underwent intense torture, and from there he came to Carthage where Cyprian ordained him a deacon, though Celerinus was reluctant to receive ordination until he was persuaded by a heavenly vision in the night.[31] The extreme nature of his suffering may have given him the premature title of martyr but he would become a full-fledged martyr later, alongside two uncles and an aunt. His sisters, choosing not to follow his *via dolorosa*, sacrificed, though they later repented and demonstrated their penance through prison ministry. Celerinus's story conveys the complexity of persecution in the third century—within the same family there were martyrs, confessors, and the so-called lapsed.

The lapsed controversy

Those who traded their faith for their physical life by offering some level of sacrifice, or by bribing an official to forge a

---

29 Cyprian, *On the Lapsed* 8.

30 Cyprian, *On the Lapsed* 8.

31 Cyprian, *Letter* 33.1.

document that said they sacrificed, were styled the 'lapsed' (*lapsi*). Allen Brent does a fine job of explaining the different levels of lapsing: 'To Cyprian all who so sacrificed (*sacrificati*) were apostates . . . . Those who had been allowed to offer incense (*thurificati*) with no animal sacrifices . . . were placed in the same category as were those who bribed the magistrate (*libellatici*) in order to obtain a certificate (*libellus*) that said they had sacrificed when they had not.'[32] Thus there were three major categories of the lapsed: *libellatici*, *thurificati*, and *sacrificati*, and each level of lapsing warranted its own punishment. Of course, there was one other way to avoid sacrificing—one could flee, as Cyprian did.[33]

Cyprian escaped the city and went into hiding at the outset of the persecution. He justified his behavior by appealing to Jesus and Paul in Scripture, both of whom fled persecution at times. Moss says, 'Other than Clement [of Alexandria] and Cyprian . . . evidence for Christians exiling themselves or lapsing by offering sacrifice comes from those who polemicize against these practices. Only with Clement and Cyprian do we begin to see exegetical and rational foundations for self-exile.'[34] The arch-polemicist against fleeing was Tertullian, who had written a treatise about a half century before called *On Flight in Times of Persecution*, condemning those who scattered when persecution came. Tertullian was clear: 'Men should not flee in [persecution]. For if persecution proceeds from God, in no way will it be our duty to flee from what has God as its author.'[35] Not only does God appoint suffering for the trial of faith,[36] but Tertullian reasons, 'He who fears to suffer, cannot belong to Him who suffered.'[37]

---

32   Brent, *Cyprian*, 7–8.

33   Although, as Brent observes, 'Cyprian was to insist that flight and exile were in themselves forms of martyrdom, and not examples of lapsing' (Brent, *Cyprian and Roman Carthage*, 10).

34   Moss, *The Myth of Persecution*, 155.

35   Tertullian, *On Flight in Persecution* 4.

36   Tertullian, *On Flight in Persecution* 2.

37   Tertullian, *On Flight in Persecution* 14.

Regardless of what Tertullian said, Cyprian fled. He thought it best to remain under deep cover and not to show himself rashly in public.[38] It would be foolish to parade about in public when there were people looking for figures of high profile, especially because so many other leaders had already been killed.[39] The sheep needed their shepherd. From his place of exile, Cyprian frequently wrote to the presbyters in Carthage in order to retain his leadership.[40] Peter Hinchliff suggested, 'It may be that he was convinced that the church in Carthage would only survive if his hand remained at the helm, even if from a distance.'[41] Not everyone in Carthage interpreted Cyprian's flight as a leadership move for their benefit; rather, they thought he was a coward who was trying to protect his own skin when the pressure ticked up a few degrees. Cyprian's letters during this time can come across desperate, as he tries to maintain a tight grip on the reigns from afar while those who were directly challenging his leadership were present in the city. Cyprian urged the presbyters and deacons in Carthage 'to discharge there both [their] office and [his], that there may be nothing wanting either to discipline or diligence.'[42] Despite his pleas, rivals to his authority rose up in the church over how to proceed with the lapsed. Cyprian remained hidden until the persecution had died down, returning shortly before Easter 251.

Meanwhile, Decius never stopped being a soldier and was slain by the Goths at the Battle of Abritus in an ill-advised skirmish in the eastern regions of the Empire (modern day Bulgaria). The persecution he had started had already begun to fizzle out early

---

38   Cyprian, *Letter* 5.1.

39   Even the Roman clergy came to Cyprian's defense, persuading those in Carthage that Cyprian 'acted quite rightly, because he is a person of eminence' (*Letter* 2.1). Exposing himself would be reckless, both for himself and for the church, and they would know since their bishop was martyred.

40   *Letters* 5–43 were written during Decius's persecution.

41   Peter Hinchliff, *Cyprian of Carthage and the Unity of the Christian Church* (London: Geoffrey Chapman, 1974), p. 47.

42   Cyprian, *Letter* 4.1.

in 251. As soon as persecution cooled, controversy flared up, even though there was plenty of smoke during the season of trial. The events can be difficult to unravel because of the various factions, changes in leadership, and the disputes between Rome and Carthage, but the essence of controversy centered on two questions—should those who had lapsed be readmitted to the church? If so, under what conditions?

The first question divided the church into two main factions—the *laxists*, who thought a repentant attitude was enough to readmit the fallen, and the *rigorists*, who believed that the breach of faith was so deep that the lapsed could not be readmitted except perhaps on their deathbeds, but even then it was not a sure thing. Carthage leaned to the laxist side of the debate, believing that those who repented should be allowed back into the church before submitting to a season of penance. The leader of this movement in Carthage was a deacon named Felicissimus.[43] Felicissimus wanted confessors, those who testified for their faith and were tortured and/or imprisoned but not martyred, to grant a 'certificate of peace' (*libelli pacis*) to the lapsed. A confessor's endorsement carried such weight because he had endured hardship for his faith—if he was willing to grant absolution, who was the bishop to stop it, especially a bishop who fled and did not subject himself to torture?

The confessors posed a unique challenge. On the one hand, the confessors had demonstrated a strong faith by refusing to sacrifice and were willing to suffer martyrdom. On the other hand, they were often lay people in the church who did not, or even could not, understand the ramifications their actions had on the church. They meant well, but they were inadvertently causing problems. Cyprian mentions the confessor Lucian, and after glowing about his faith, says that he was 'little established

---

43 See especially *Letter* 39, which has been entitled, 'To the People, Concerning Five Schismatic Presbyters of the Faction of Felicissimus.' Cyprian wanted to warn the people about the 'ancient poison against [his] episcopate.'

in the reading of the Lord's word,' and 'unskilled.'[44] Yet Cyprian knew that he could not simply reject the letters of the martyrs. Mob rule had already deemed that these letters carried with them the power to forgive. Cyprian struck a deal that these letters could be used to give restoration to those who were dying, but he held out that the others needed a season of penance.

Although Cyprian had desired to wait to the end of the persecution to figure out how to restore the fallen, those who were left to lead in the city, like Felicissimus, were forced to make difficult decisions regarding the lapsed and thought they could not wait that long. Nor did they want to. Advice from their absent bishop fell on deaf ears. The presbyters and deacons in Carthage held that a letter from a confessor about to be martyred could absolve the lapsed from sin. The bishop knew the havoc this could create, effectively becoming a 'get out of penance free card', thereby foregoing a critical step in the process of repentance. And this is precisely what happened. A black market of sorts developed around the trafficking of martyrs' letters.[45] Some of these letters even mysteriously appeared after a confessor was martyred, which made authenticating these letters a matter of church purity.

Thus, Cyprian could hold his tongue no longer. He felt as though these presbyters had overstepped their bounds, disregarding the gospel and forgetting God's future judgment, because the divine precepts were 'relaxed by certain presbyters, who consider neither the fear of God nor the honor of the bishop.'[46] In addition to their neglect of church order, these factious leaders were making a mockery of the sacraments. Due to their hasty process of reconciliation, there were lapsed partaking of the Eucharist who had not made proper confession

---

44 Cyprian, *Letter* 22.1.

45 Burns, *Cyprian the Bishop*, 2-3.

46 Cyprian, *Letter* 10.1. *Letters* 8-12 deal with Cyprian's frustration over the presbyters in Carthage readmitting people into the church prematurely.

and had not walked through the process of penitence.[47] Sacrificers returned from the altar of Satan to the holy place of God reeking of sacrificed meat, and then had the audacity to touch holy things with their profane hands.[48] Cyprian claimed that by allowing this to happen, the presbyters were in direct conflict with Scripture, such as when Paul said, 'You cannot drink the cup of the Lord and the cup of demons' (1 Cor 10:21). It is unthinkable that the lapsed should be brought back into the fold while confessors remained in prison, and while certain people were in exile and deprived of their home, obviously thinking of himself.[49]

What motivated Cyprian against giving immediate clemency to the lapsed? Did Cyprian believe that repentance alone is insufficient to grant for forgiveness and restoration? Was it a lack of grace? Was it a matter of control? These do not seem to be his motives. Cyprian's heart towards the lapsed was not that of a punitive bishop who wanted to bar genuine believers from the church, but that of a loving shepherd who longed for their repentance. In a letter written during the first summer of the persecution, Cyprian was concerned that the summer heat would bring an increase of 'heavy sickness' and that some of the lapsed might die before being readmitted into the church. He implored the leaders who remained in Carthage to lay hands for repentance on the lapsed and allow those who had received a certificate from a martyr to regain entry into the church before they died. In fact, no one who sought the mercy of the Lord on their deathbed should be denied. He wished for the leaders of the church to 'cherish also by your presence the rest of the people who are lapsed, and cheer them by your consolation, that they may not fail of the faith of God's mercy.'[50]

---

47   Cyprian makes this case both in *Letters* 9 and 10.
48   Cyprian, *On the Lapsed* 15.
49   Cyprian, *Letter* 13.2.
50   Cyprian, *Letter* 12.2.

Cyprian's strict standards actually flowed out of concern for the lapsed. To Cyprian, granting forgiveness too soon was detrimental to the soul of the person who had denied Christ. To be sure, forgiveness could be extended, both from Christ and the Church, but if the Church was too lenient in granting forgiveness, it would not inspire courage in future persecutions and it would defame those who suffered and died. Ultimately, it was for the good of the lapsed to undergo some form of penance to demonstrate the sincerity of their repentance. Despite Cyprian's desire to reincorporate the lapsed into fellowship, even he held out that those who sacrificed should have to wait for their deathbed to receive full forgiveness.

As far as Cyprian was concerned, Felicissimus and company instituted another stage of persecution. Those who cut themselves off from Christ when they lapsed were now prevented from returning to Him rightly. Cyprian writes,

> He who has denied Christ should not appeal for mercy to the same Christ whom he had denied; that after the fault of the crime, repentance also should be taken away; and that the Lord should not be appeased through bishops and priests, but that the Lord's priests being forsaken, a new tradition of a sacrilegious appointment should arise, contrary to the evangelical discipline.[51]

Appealing to Christ for mercy was tantamount to seeking forgiveness from the bishops, who are the heirs of Christ. Furthermore, repentance is not simply a sorrowful feeling of the heart but it is a demonstration of contrition over a long enough period of time that genuine remorse could be seen by all, or at least the bishop.

This controversy was not contained to Carthage. Those in Rome were simultaneously experiencing the problem of how to handle the lapsed. The bishop's seat had remained vacant after Fabian was martyred, but in March 251 Rome elected Cornelius,

---

51 Cyprian, *Letter* 39.3.

a laxist, to fill the seat. Soon after this Novatian, a rigorist, was elected as a rival bishop of the Roman church. Novatian was a rigorist to the point that he thought those who had lapsed could never be accepted back into the church, not even on their deathbeds.[52] Both bishops began writing letters to seek support for their own claim to the bishopric. Carthage sent a delegation to Rome to sort through the dispute, and upon their return, backed Cornelius.

The conflict was only to worsen for Cyprian. Two rival bishops set up camp in Carthage representing the extreme positions. Novatian, upset that Cyprian had sided with Cornelius, sent Maximus, who had been a presbyter in Rome, to be the rigorist bishop in Carthage, while Fortunatus, a former presbyter of Cyprian's, was installed as the laxist bishop. As Burns notes, 'Cyprian and his colleagues were under assault from both sides.'[53]

Cyprian's solution was to steer a middle course between the rigorists and the laxists. As hinted above, his answer to the second question posed, namely, under what conditions can the repentant be allowed back into the church, was penance. Penance was whole-hearted repentance made visible to others that provided atonement for sins committed after initial faith and baptism. His treatise *On the Lapsed* set forth his balanced approach to readmitting the lapsed. 'Repent abundantly,' Cyprian urged, 'prove the sorrow of a grieving and lamenting mind.'[54] Not all those who had lapsed were demonstrating a contrite heart. How, he asked, can a person be considered repentant who is visiting bath houses with women and who is frequenting lavish banquets, instead of entreating the Lord in fasting and weeping?[55] Genuine remorse that fit the crime was

---

52 Cyprian believed Novatian's greatest crime was schism in that he attempted 'to cut and tear the one body of the Catholic Church' (*Letter* 40.2).

53 Burns, *Cyprian*, 8. Burns provides a very helpful overview of this controversy on pp. 6-9.

54 Cyprian, *On the Lapsed* 32.

55 Cyprian, *On the Lapsed* 30.

needed. God is merciful and will forgive, but only if a person undertakes appropriate steps. Practically speaking, penance most often consisted of prayer, fasting, mourning, and almsgiving.

The Catholic doctrine of penance was born out of the lapsed controversy, but the full dogma of penance must not be read back into Cyprian. Protestants have always been quick to criticize the practice of penance, and rightly so, because penance assumes that there is an insufficiency in Christ's atonement that must be made up for with good works. If Christ's atonement was efficacious to pay for every sin of the believer, then what is the purpose of penance? However, if penance is seen as visible repentance to the believing community as part of the process of sanctification, then could there be value in the concept, even if the word itself has many problems? For Cyprian, penance seems to have both functions—that is, it both purges sins committed after initial faith and baptism, and it serves to demonstrate genuine repentance.[56] The latter is something that evangelicals can embrace; the former must be rejected outright.

I would suggest that evangelicals are already re-appropriating this idea in some respects. Mark Dever has spent his ministry defining the 'nine marks' of a healthy church, one of which is church discipline. Dever writes, 'If someone who claims to be a Christian refuses to live as a Christian should live, we need to follow what Paul said and, for the glory of God and for that person's own good, we need to exclude him or her from membership in the church.'[57] Discipline is for the good of the person, the health of the church, and the glory of God. No doubt Dever would avoid the word penance, but the idea of church discipline does seem to capture an important facet of Cyprian's view of penance. Does a believer not have to amend his or her ways before being brought back into the church? Is communion not denied them? Is the church not saying that a person should

---

56 See chapter 4 for a more detailed discussion.

57 Mark Dever, *Nine Marks of a Healthy Church* (Wheaton: Crossway, 2004), p. 171.

fear for his soul if he is under the discipline of the church? For the sake of the soul discipline is practiced to bring about restoration. In my estimation, this is the primary aim behind Cyprian's view of penance. Again, the term is tarnished beyond recovery, but the practice itself, so long as it is not thought to atone for sins, is necessary for the health of the church.

Cyprian's middle way was not the final gavel strike in the controversy. Those who disagreed on either end of the spectrum continued to cause trouble. Further proof that the church had not settled the issue was the Donatist controversy that erupted after the Great Persecution of Diocletian. Donatists had the same streak of rigorism that the Novatianists had before them. Augustine still had to deal with Donatists in Hippo one hundred years after Diocletian's persecution had ended.[58]

Since the time of Constantine the western church has not faced the same type of systemic persecution and so it is impossible to say just how similar the controversy would be if it resumed, though I suspect the church would divide again along similar lines.[59] In the event that persecution returns, should the church take a rigorist, laxist, or middle approach? Given the current state of superficiality and lukewarmness among western evangelicals, it seems many would favor the laxist approach. However, it would be best for the church to consider Cyprian's middle path and ask for a period of visible repentance—neither as a means of atoning sins nor as a legalistic hoop through which the guilty must jump, nor even as a shaming process, but as a way to shepherd the souls of those who commit the grave offense of denying Christ, who said, 'whoever denies me before men, I also will deny before my Father who is in heaven' (Matt 10:33; cf. 2 Tim 2:12).

---

58   See the following works from Augustine: *On Baptism, Against the Donatists*; *Answer to Letters of Petilian, Bishop of Cirta*; and, *The Correction of the Donatists*.

59   Of course, there have been plenty of large scale persecutions, such as English Baptists from 1660-1688 and the treatment of believers in Nazi Germany, and in these instances the controversy has followed similar fault lines.

Rebaptism

The lapsed controversy set the stage for the next battle of Cyprian's ministry over the issue of rebaptism, which was not so much how to handle the lapsed as it was how to handle schismatics. Novatian and his faction had torn off one side of the church and Fortunatus and his faction had torn the church from the other side. Though, for Cyprian, this was not a dispute within the church—these were factious churches that split from the true church. Thus the question was raised whether the catholic church could recognize baptisms conducted by schismatics, or should the church rebaptize? Suppose, for instance, a person baptized in Novatian's camp broke from that church and wanted to join a fellowship in communion with Cyprian. Is this person's baptism by a Novatianist bishop legitimate or do they need to pass through the waters again, since their initial baptism was conducted by a 'profane washing'?[60]

This question about rebaptism was not new. Those in the second century had to deal with a similar problem, namely, with groups like the Marcionites who held heretical views of God and Jesus.[61] Regarding baptism from heretical groups, Cyprian said,

> For if we and heretics have one faith, we may also have one grace. If the Patripassians, Anthropians, Valentinians, Apelletians, Ophites, Marcionites, and other pests, and swords, and poisons of heretics for subverting the truth, confess the same Father, the same Son, the same Holy Ghost, the same Church with us, they may also have one baptism if they have also one faith.[62]

The problem, of course, is that their faiths were entirely different. In an outstanding statement on the Trinity (a word first used in Latin by Tertullian)[63] Cyprian writes,

---

60   Cyprian, *Letter* 75.1.

61   Cyprian, *Letter* 72.4.

62   Cyprian, *Letter* 72.4.

63   Tertullian, *Against Praxeas*.

Does Marcion then maintain the Trinity? Does he then assert the same Father, the Creator as we do? Does he know the same Son, Christ born of the Virgin Mary, who as the Word was made flesh, who bore our sins, who conquered death by dying, who by Himself first of all originated the resurrection of the flesh, and showed to His disciples that He had risen in the same flesh? *Widely different* is the faith with Marcion, and, moreover, with the other heretics nay, with them there is nothing but perfidy, and blasphemy, and contention, which is hostile to holiness and truth.[64]

Invoking a Trinitarian formula means nothing if the Trinity is not understood in the same way. If a group believed in the Trinity rightly, and if they believed in the true, apostolic church and the rightful bishops, then their baptisms would be valid. But if they believed these things, then they were not an aberrant sect. Surely, Cyprian reasoned, baptism from these sects could not be accepted because their doctrine was outside the bounds of orthodoxy.

In arguing this way, Cyprian swam upstream against tradition. The position of the church up to this point had been that as long as a person was baptized in the Triune name, then the baptism was valid regardless of the officiant.[65] If the person baptizing mattered, then every baptism by a bishop who later apostatized was invalid. However, those on Cyprian's side of the issue would ask how a baptism could be legitimate when administered by someone outside of the church? The new

---

64 Cyprian, *Letter* 72.5, emphasis added.

65 This is too early for the view of *ex opere operato* ('by the work performed') or even *ex opere operantis* ('by the act of one who performs it'), which teaches that the sacraments function irrespective of faith or that the sacrament is effective because of the one who performs it, respectively. Yet Brent recognizes that 'the kernel of the later principle [*ex opere operantis*] is expressed in Stephen's theology' (*Cyprian and Roman Carthage*, 306). The point in this controversy was whether or not the person administering the sacrament assented to the right faith, which is closer to *ex opere operantis*. Cyprian is clear that 'when [baptism] is done in the Church, where the faith both of the receiver and giver is sound, all things hold and may be consummated and perfected by the majesty of the Lord and by the truth of faith' (*Letter* 75.12).

challenge was about schismatics more than heretics. Those in the rigorist and laxist camps would have articulated their belief in the Trinity the same way Cyprian did. Was their baptism valid then? Cyprian answered that their baptism was invalid because they had separated from the catholic church.

Baptism belongs to the true church and so must be administered by those in the church. Cyprian responded to a letter from Magnus (*Letter* 75), about whom we know only what we can glean from this letter, which started the debate. From the opening of the letter Cyprian replied, 'I answer that no heretics and schismatics at all have any power or right [to baptize].'[66] The logic was sound. Novatian was not in the true church and thus was not a real bishop; therefore, he could not baptize.[67] There is only one Lord, one church, and one baptism, and Christ gave Himself to wash (baptism in Cyprian's mind) his bride (Eph 4:4-6).[68] 'Rebels and enemies,' among whom he numbered Novatian, 'who forge false altars, and lawless priesthoods, and sacrilegious sacrifices' can have no part in administering the sacraments.[69]

The controversy began over what to do with those like Novatian who had departed from the church, but the debate soon caught the attention of Stephen, the new bishop of Rome

---

66 Cyprian, *Letter* 75.1. Recently the traditional dating of Cyprian's writings during the rebaptism controversy has been debated. Burns argues that the letter to Magnus (*Letter* 75), which has typically been used as the start of the debate, should come after the synodal letters of 256 (*Cyprian*, 100-31). Stuart Hall, representing the opposing view, disregards the common view that the revision of *On the Unity of the Church* (see next chapter) has anything to do with the rebaptism controversy and so dates the work at 252 ('The Versions of Cyprian's *De Unitate*, 4-5: Bévenot's Dating Revisited,' *Journal of Theological Studies*, n.s. 55 [2004], p. 146). For an assessment of these views and a mediating position, see Karl Shuve, 'Cyprian of Carthage's Writings from the Rebaptism Controversy: Two Revisionary Proposals Reconsidered,' *Journal of Theological Studies*, n.s. 61.2 (2010) pp. 627-643. Shuve likely did not have access to Brent's monograph published in the same year as his article. Brent takes the letter to Magnus as the start of the debate (*Cyprian and Roman Carthage*, 295), with whom I agree.

67 Cyprian, *Letter* 75.3.

68 Cyprian, *Letter* 75.2. Cf. Cyprian, *Letter* 73.11.

69 Cyprian, *Letter* 75.1.

who had been installed in May 254. A total of three councils were held in Carthage to discuss this matter, of which the first two were inconclusive. The third council, however, attended by eighty-seven African bishops confirmed Cyprian's position on September 1, 256.[70] They decided that those baptized by heretics or schismatics must be rebaptized in order to join the catholic church.[71] According to Eusebius, Cyprian was the first one to argue this.[72]

Stephen followed the traditional line of thinking that the status of the baptizer did not matter so long as the correct baptismal formula was spoken. All that was necessary for a person seeking admittance into a catholic fellowship was the bishop laying hands on the person. Stephen appealed to John the Baptist for support of his position.[73] John came baptizing for repentance, but his baptism lacked the Holy Spirit. Those John baptized were able to receive the Holy Spirit later with the laying on of hands. Cyprian in turn pointed to Acts 19 where Paul engaged believers in Ephesus who were baptized by John but had never even heard of the Holy Spirit. Paul's solution was to baptize them in the name of the Lord Jesus because they had

---

70 See Brent, *Cyprian and Roman Carthage*, 17–18 for a quick overview. It was the custom in the ante-Nicene era to hold regional synods. Geoffrey Dunn notes, 'The "rebaptism" controversy demonstrates that in a church that saw itself as a collection of communities and that lacked a centralized authority, uniformity of Christian life and practice was established by building consensus among bishops. Synods provided the ideal forum in which to achieve that' ('Validity of Baptism and Ordination in the African Response to the "Rebaptism" Crisis: Cyprian of Carthage's Synod of Spring 256,' *Theological Studies* 67 [2006]: 273–74). This fact, along with the ensuing conflict with Stephen, demonstrates that the Roman bishop was not thought to be the supreme bishop in the third century.

71 Geoffrey Dunn, 'Validity of Baptism and Ordination in the African Response to the "Rebaptism" Crisis,' pp. 258–59.

72 Eusebius, *Church History* 7.3.

73 At least this seems to be what Stephen argued. We do not have any direct correspondence from Stephen, only what is mediated through Cyprian. The bulk of the controversy can be found in Cyprian's *Letters* 69–75. Allen Brent has tried to reconstruct the controversy, and I have summarized him here. See especially Brent, *Cyprian and Roman Carthage*, pp. 300–307.

never received true baptism. Stephen then supplied the counter-example of Philip and the Samaritans. Furthermore, Stephen pointed to the power that Jesus' name has when it is invoked, thus making subsequent baptism superfluous. At the Council of Jerusalem in Acts 15, Jews and Gentiles who invoke the name of the Lord are saved. In the same way, heretics or schismatics who were baptized in the name of Jesus are like those Jews and Gentiles who invoked Jesus' name. In other words, as Brent summarizes, 'the heretics and schismatics are, therefore, in the same position as those who first met Jesus without receiving the Holy Spirit, or the pagans over whom the name of Jesus is first invoked.'[74]

Cyprian passionately disagreed. The reason a bishop lays hands on the one baptized is to signify the reception of the Holy Spirit. Those who do not have the Holy Spirit to begin with are not able to baptize and impart the Spirit.[75] For this reason Haykin observes, 'This controversy is usually described as a controversy about rebaptism, though, in many ways, the real issue at stake had to do not so much with baptism as with the Spirit.'[76] If we dig deeper still, the bedrock of the controversy was a different understanding of the church, her unity, and her integrity.[77] Those who started their own church separated themselves from the true church, the rightful bishop, the saving sacraments, and the indwelling of the Holy Spirit. In a word,

---

74 Brent, *Cyprian and Roman Carthage*, 305. Brent gives a very important aside for his modern reader. Words were alive in the ancient worldview. Blessings and curses, for instance, once spoken could not be taken back—they lived on as an extension, or fragment, of a person's spirit. Thus, to invoke the Lord's name was significant. 'Once God's word has been uttered in human speech, or expressed concretely and visibly in a prophetic sign, it possesses that overwhelming divine force that accomplishes God's unchanging purpose' (Brent, *Cyprian and Roman Carthage*, p. 306).

75 Cyprian, *Letter* 75.10.

76 Michael Haykin, 'The Holy Spirit in Cyprian's *To Donatus*,' p. 324.

77 Allen Brent, *Cyprian and Roman Carthage*, pp. 290–91.

schismatics had separated themselves from salvation. The rift was never resolved because Stephen died as a martyr in 257 and Cyprian similarly died not long after in 258.

In less than a decade as bishop, Cyprian had faced two persecutions (Decius and Valerian) and two controversies (Lapsed and Rebaptism). Nearly all his writings were framed by these events and thus carried a polemical tone. At the core of all his writings, as they were filtered through controversies, was his concern of the church.

3

CYPRIAN AND THE CHURCH

The writings of Cyprian have surfaced time and again when the church is embroiled in controversy, perhaps no more so than during the Reformation. In the scales of the sixteenth century were placed justification by faith on one side, and the unity of the church on the other, and church leaders at the time struggled to know to which side they should cast their weight.[1] As loud as Luther trumpeted justification by faith, there were those in the Catholic Church who would, with equal vehemence, chant back the unity of the church, though it should be noted that Luther did not wish to fracture the church. Many in the Roman Church believed that Cyprian was an ally who had pronounced the definitive word on the church, even championing the Roman pontiff over a millennium before the Reformation. Luther did not see it this way—he too saw an ally in Cyprian. In a showdown between Luther and a Catholic bishop, perhaps Albert of Brandenburg, Archbishop of Mainz, Cyprian became the topic and Luther the victor.

---

1 B. B. Warfield famously said, 'For the Reformation, inwardly considered, was just the ultimate triumph of Augustine's doctrine of grace over Augustine's doctrine of the Church' (Warfield, *Calvin and Augustine* [Philadelphia: The Presbyterian and Reformed Publishing Co., n.d.], p. 322). The Augustinian view of the church is really the Cyprianic view of the church.

I know a great archbishop, whom I shall not name, who had a high opinion of St. Cyprian, the holy bishop and martyr, and read a bit in his books [to arm himself] against the Lutherans, intending thereby entirely to overthrow them. But when it was pointed out to him that in the books of the same St. Cyprian it is written that the holy Christian Church is found not only in Rome but in every corner of the world, he said, 'If I had known that Cyprian taught that, I would have had his books burned as those of a heretic.' And when the passage in the book was shown to him, he threw Cyprian and his book away and would no longer read the heretic.[2]

How had this bishop come to misread Cyprian? The answer is that the Catholic Church had co-opted Cyprian, especially in the Middle Ages, to bolster belief in the primacy of the Roman bishop. It was thought that Cyprian had argued that the Roman pontiff alone was the direct heir of Peter, to whom Jesus gave authority in Matthew 16. One prime example was that of Pope Boniface VIII, who in an aggressive power play against King Philip IV of France (r. 1285–1314), issued a papal bull in 1302 called *Unam Sanctam*, which displayed the height of papal arrogance.[3]

Urged by faith, we are obliged to believe and to maintain that the Church is one, holy, catholic, and also apostolic. We believe

---

[2] Luther, 'Preface to Lazarus Spengler, *Brief Excerpt from the Papal Laws* (1530),' in *Luther's Works*, ed. and trans. James M. Estes, 59:275.

[3] Literally it means 'One Holy,' after the first two words of the Latin text. The French did not take kindly to this bull and sent men to capture the Pope in order to bring him to France to stand trial, primarily over the suspicious abdication of his predecessor, Pope Celestine V, along with Celestine's wrongful imprisonment at the hands of Boniface. Boniface was held in captivity in his quarters and before they could extradite him back to France, locals were able to overtake the captors. Ultimately this kidnapping was unsuccessful, but Boniface died shortly after. One historian summed up Boniface's life this way, 'As a wolf he entered, as a lion he ruled, as a dog he finished' (William Thorne, *Chronicle of Saint Augustine's Abbey Canterbury*, trans. A. H. Davis [Oxford: Oxford University Press, 1934], p. 385, quoted from Roger Collins, *Keepers of the Keys of Heaven: A History of the Papacy* [New York: Basic Books, 2009], p. 281).

in her firmly and we confess with simplicity that outside of her there is neither salvation nor the remission of sins, as the Spouse in the Canticles proclaims: 'One is my dove, my perfect one'. . . . In her then is one Lord, one faith, one baptism. There had been at the time of the deluge only one ark of Noah, prefiguring the one Church. . . . We venerate this Church as one. . . . This is the tunic of the Lord, the seamless tunic, which was not rent but which was cast by lot. Therefore, of the one and only Church there is one body and one head, not two heads like a monster; that is, Christ and the Vicar of Christ, Peter and the successor of Peter . . . . in this Church and in its power are two swords; namely, the spiritual and temporal. . . . Certainly the one who denies that the temporal sword is in the power of Peter has not listened well to the word of the Lord. . . . Hence we must recognize the more clearly that spiritual power surpasses in dignity and in nobility any temporal power whatever, as spiritual things surpass the temporal.[4]

There is one church, just as there was one, seamless tunic of Christ and just as there was one ark that carried Noah and his family to safety. This one Church was given two swords, the spiritual and the temporal, asserting that the Catholic Church, and specifically the Pope, has ultimate power, both in the church and in secular society. The ultimate appeal to papal authority comes in the last line of the bull—'Furthermore, we declare, we proclaim, we define that it is absolutely necessary for salvation that every human creature be subject to the Roman Pontiff.' Three successive verbs (declare [*declaramus*], proclaim [*pronunciamus*], define [*definimus*]) were used to accentuate the point of the document, namely, that the Pope has ultimate authority and that salvation depends on acknowledging his supremacy.

Several of the stronger statements from the bull are lifted straight from Cyprian's own writings, which is why the bishop of

---

4   This translation comes from Bob van Cleef's dissertation in 1927 from the Catholic University of America. This translation can be found at http://www.newadvent.org/library/ docs_bo08us.htm; accessed January 21, 2016.

Mainz thought he had a sure friend in the bishop from Carthage. After all, it was Cyprian who boasted his own strong claims, such as, 'There is no salvation outside of the church,'[5] and 'you cannot have God as your Father if you do not have the Church as your Mother.'[6] Regarding the primacy of bishops, Cyprian said, 'The glory of the Church is the glory of the bishop.'[7] Was Boniface on track when he exerted his claim over the world? Was this not the logical flow of Cyprian's argument? Luther did not think so, and it seems that Luther had a better handle on Cyprian than his opponent, which is why the bishop decided to burn Cyprian's books instead of to read them. This grab at authority is hardly what Cyprian had in mind when he wrote on the nature of the church. As is the case in many things in Cyprian's writings, later appropriation and disfigurement of his thought should not be read back into his original ideas.

Defining the church is Cyprian's legacy. At the center of Cyprian—his very life, hope, and salvation—is the church. He could not separate the church from the Christian, for one could not exist without the other. In a letter to Antonianus concerning the schism between Cornelius and Novatian, Cyprian stated plainly, 'he who is not in the Church of Christ is not a Christian.'[8] Connection to the authentic, visible church is vital for salvation. This idea led Cyprian to the work that won him a significant place in history.

On the unity of the Church

Upon return from his self-imposed exile in 251, Cyprian wrote his most important work *De Unitate Ecclesiae*, or *On the Unity of the Church*. The year and a half of persecution

---

5   Cyprian, *Letter* 72.21.

6   Cyprian, *On the Unity of the Church* 6. Both of these will be looked at in greater detail below.

7   Cyprian, *Letter* 6.1.

8   Cyprian, *Letter* 51.24.

revealed significant cracks in the church's infrastructure, as the foundation of the church, the bishops, were challenged in their leadership, both by Roman authorities that sought their blood, and by church schismatics who sought their seats. Cyprian's greatest fear was the latter, those who slipped into the church wearing sheep's clothing but were ravenous wolves. In the opening section, Cyprian writes, 'The enemy is more to be feared and to be guarded against, when he creeps on us secretly; when, deceiving by the appearance of peace, he steals forward by hidden approaches, whence also he has received the name of the Serpent.'[9] Cyprian wanted to lay out in bold the nature and the structure of the church that Christ had provided in order to protect the flock from these serpents who slithered in unnoticed and spread their venomous ideas. *On the Unity of the Church* was Cyprian's solution, written specifically against Novation and his group, whose careless lust for power threatened the indivisibility of the church. For at least a thousand years, Cyprian would give shape to the structure of the church through this short book.

Cyprian's argument rested on two pillars—the nature and the structure of the church. Regarding the nature of the church, the church is one. Regarding the structure of the church, Jesus built His church on the foundation of the bishops. In the end these were mutually dependent. The structure is what held together the nature, since the church is only one when the authority of the bishops is recognized.

Unity is at the center of the nature of the church. Cyprian argues this from texts like Song of Solomon, where Solomon says to his bride, 'My dove, my perfect one, is the only one, the only one of her mother, pure to her who bore her' (Song 6:9).[10] Solomon's song has been understood as an allegory of God and His people, possibly since before Jesus was born in a stable and the church was born at Pentecost, but it was definitely interpreted

---

9   Cyprian, *On the Unity of the Church* 1.

10 Cyprian, *Letter* 75.2.

as a metaphor of Christ and the Church from early on in the church age.[11] What stood out to him was the repetition of 'one,' which is repeated three times in this verse. From here he makes the logical step from the Song to Ephesians 4:4-6: 'There is one body and one Spirit—just as you were called to the one hope that belongs to your call—one Lord, one faith, one baptism, one God and Father of all, who is over all and through all and in all.' Even though the Church is spread around geographically, she still remains one body.

Cyprian employs an array of illustrations from nature to illumine the oneness of the Church.

> As there are many rays of the sun, but one light; and many branches of a tree, but one strength based in its tenacious root; and since from one spring flow many streams, although the multiplicity seems diffused in the liberality of an overflowing abundance, yet the unity does not allow a division of light; break a branch from a tree—when broken, it will not be able to bud; cut off the stream from its fountain, and that which is cut off dries up. Thus also the Church, shone over with the light of the Lord, sheds forth her rays over the whole world, yet is one light which is everywhere diffused, nor is the unity of the body separated.[12]

---

11 Scholars debate whether or not Jewish sources prior to the Church read Song of Solomon allegorically. Weston Fields, for instance, argues that 'there is no record of allegorization in the earliest period' of Jewish writings ('Early and Medieval Jewish Interpretation of the Song of Songs,' *Grace Theological Journal* 1 [1980]: 222). Christians undoubtedly interpreted the Song allegorically as Christ's love for His beloved church. Joseph Carola claims that it was 'Cyprian whose ecclesiological application of the Canticle established the standard of future discourse in the African mezzogiorno' (*Augustine of Hippo: The Role of the Laity in Ecclesial Reconciliation* [Rome: Editrice Pontificia Università Gregoriana, 2005], p. 125). This penchant to allegorize the Song carried over into the Middle Ages when figures like Bede and Bernard of Clairvaux offered their interpretations of Solomon's erotic poem. Even in the Reformation era, John Calvin was so strongly persuaded that an allegorical reading was the only legitimate hermeneutic for the Song that he ran Sebastian Castellio out of town when Castellio rendered a literal reading to the text (see Bruce Gordon, *Calvin* [New Haven: Yale University Press, 2009], p. 157).

12 Cyprian, *On the Unity of the Church* 5.

There is an organic connection between the ray of light and the sun, the branch and the root, the stream and the fountain, that ceases to exist if the contingent element is removed from the necessary element.[13] There is only one sun. If you stop receiving light from the one sun, you cannot turn to another sun to be warmed. Likewise, once a person has separated herself from the church, she has separated herself from the very thing that brought life. The schismatics foolishly think that they can break a branch from the tree, replant it in new soil, and expect it to bud and bear fruit. This is utterly impossible, says Cyprian, for once the branch is snapped from the root the tree shrivels and dies. No life can spring from a rootless branch. The root of the church, starting from its inception, is Christ, which branched into the apostles and then out into the bishops.

To strengthen the language even more against the schismatics, Cyprian states, 'The spouse of Christ cannot be adulterous.'[14] Leaving the Church to establish one's own church is tantamount to saying that the church can commit adultery on her husband. It is in this context that he makes one of his legendary dictums about the church.

> Whoever is separated from the Church and is joined to an adulteress, is separated from the promises of the Church; nor can he who forsakes the Church of Christ attain to the rewards of Christ. He is a stranger; he is profane; he is an enemy. *He can no longer have God for his Father, who has not the Church for his mother* (*Habere iam non potest Deum patrem qui ecclesiam non habet matrem*).[15]

The reason that he began his book by speaking of deception is because there are many who would claim to have God as their

---

13 Several of these illustrations became critical in the Trinitarian debates just over a half-century after Cyprian's martyrdom.

14 Cyprian, *On the Unity of the Church* 6.

15 Cyprian, *On the Unity of the Church* 6, emphasis added. Latin text from *L'Unité de L'Église*, Sources Chrétiennes, 500:188.

Father, but who have nothing to do with the one, holy, apostolic, catholic church. By separating themselves from the Church, they are adulterers, profane, and enemies of the very God whom they try to call their Father. Every person needs a mother and a father, and this is true of the Christian as well. To have God as a Father, a person must have the Church as his mother, for 'from her womb we are born, by her milk we are nourished, by her spirit we are animated.'[16]

Separating God the Father from Mother Church is like cosmic divorce, which is precisely what the schismatics were doing. Schism in the church is actually a 'worse crime' than lapsing.[17] The lapsed break under the weight of force, but the schismatic calculates his guile. By militating against God's appointment, the schismatic 'bears arms against the Church.'[18] How can one think that separation from the priests and the bishops, to whom God has entrusted the church, could lead to God's blessing? That is why schism is worse than heresy for Cyprian. Stuart Hall comments, 'Cyprian uses Paul's words to assimilate schism to heresy: to desert the Church is to corrupt the faith.'[19] Or as J. Patout Burns summarizes Cyprian on this point, 'To separate from the church was to deny Christ; to adhere to the church to confess Christ.'[20]

Cyprian believed the church is necessary for salvation. His strongest statement connecting salvation to the church came in a letter to Jubaianus concerning the rebaptism of heretics, in which he explicitly wrote, 'There is no salvation outside of

---

16   Cyprian, *On the Unity of the Church* 5. The idea of church as mother was not novel with Cyprian. This motif had been employed in part by Ignatius and Tertullian. See Bradley M. Peper, 'The Development of *Mater Ecclesia* in North African Ecclesiology' (Ph.D. diss. Vanderbilt University, 2011).

17   Cyprian, *On the Unity of the Church* 19.

18   Cyprian, *On the Unity of the Church* 17.

19   Stuart Hall, 'The Versions of Cyprian, *De Unitate*, 4–5: Bévenot's Dating Revisited,' *Journal of Theological Studies* n.s. 55 (2004): 141.

20   J. Patout Burns, 'Cyprian of Carthage,' *Expository Times* 120 (2009): 472–73.

the church' (*salus extra ecclesiam non est*).[21] It would have been inconceivable to Cyprian that a person could think of himself as a Christian and yet not be connected to the Church, since it is the Church that nourishes the heart and animates the spirit.

On this point Cyprian speaks loudly to the contemporary evangelical scene where union to the church is optional, so long as an individual has a 'personal relationship with Jesus.' The question must be raised—is connection to the visible, local church necessary for salvation? As far as Cyprian is concerned the answer is yes, since union to the church is union with Christ. We would do well to retrieve his wisdom on this point, and call for a moratorium on the hypothetical person who has placed his faith in Jesus but who seeks to live out his Christian faith disconnected from the church. While evangelicals would never want to make salvation contingent on church membership, and thus deny justification by faith alone, we must remember that Jesus Christ died for the church (Eph 5:25), and he has entrusted to her the ministry of reconciliation (2 Cor 5:18), which seems to include both the visible and invisible church. The person who professes faith in Christ, but thinks connection to the local church is superfluous, should be warned that his faith is probably not genuine. Placing oneself outside the church is like jumping from the ark into the raging sea of the world—survival is unlikely. For Cyprian it is impossible.

Keeping the church unified required structure. Cyprian maintained that unity is only possible through submission to the bishop. The lapsed may have caused conflict in the church during the persecution, but this was nothing compared to the schismatics who were threatening the essential nature of the church. The last thing Christians needed was fragmented leadership. Thankfully, Jesus had given structure to the church for times such as this—a structure centered on bishops.

---

21 Cyprian, *Letter* 72.21.

Jesus had made the structure of the church clear when He said to Peter, 'On this rock I will build my Church, and the gates of hell shall not prevail against it' (Matt 16:18).[22] For Cyprian and most of the early church, Matthew 16 was Jesus' establishment of the bishopric. Jesus appointed men upon whom He would build His one Church. In the context of Christ appointing bishops, Cyprian asks, 'Does he who does not hold this unity of the Church think that he holds the faith?'[23] The faith itself is inextricably bound to the Church, which is held together by the bishops. This is why it is important, in turn, that the bishops themselves strive to maintain a bond of unity.[24] Matthew 16 became a field of battle between Cyprian and Stephen. The issue is whether Jesus meant that Peter, and his successors in Rome, are the holders of the keys, or if Jesus was referring to all bishops.

This brings us back to a large question that was raised at the beginning of the chapter—how could Luther and a Catholic bishop both point to Cyprian in favor of their view? The answer lies in the greatest problem of *The Unity of the Church*, and one of the most significant debates in Cyprian, which hinges on a difference in the manuscripts. The text comes down in two recensions—version A and version B.[25] Version A emphasizes Peter

---

22 For an interesting reception history on this verse, see David W. Kling, *The Bible in History: How the Texts have Shaped the Time* (Oxford: Oxford University Press, 2004), pp. 45-82.

23 Cyprian, *On the Unity of the Church* 4.

24 Cyprian, *On the Unity of the Church* 5.

25 This labeling comes from D. Van den Eynde, 'La double édition du "De Unitate" de S. Cyprien,' *Revue d'histoire ecclésiastique* 29 (1933): 5-24. Another important early study came from Dom Jean Le Moyne, 'Saint Cyprien est-il bien l'auteur de la redaction brève du 'De Unitate' chapitre 4?' *Revue Bénédictine* (1953): 70-115. Dom Le Moyne recognized that the majority of scholarship now accepts that both versions come from Cyprian's hand, though some dissent still remains. The texts are also called *Primacy Text* (PT) and *Received Text* (RT). PT is so-called because it gives primacy to Peter; RT because this was the only version known until PT was rediscovered in 1563 (see Russell Murray, 'Assessing the Primacy: A Contemporary Contribution from the Writings of St. Cyprian of Carthage,' *Journal of Ecumenical Studies* 47 [2012]: 43-44).

and his successors in Rome as having primacy, whereas version B emphasizes the equality of all bishops as Peter's successors. How one understands Cyprian's role in the formation of the monarchical episcopacy relies heavily on how one resolves this debate. Does Cyprian believe that all bishops have equal power or does the Roman bishop have primacy of place?

Scholarship on this issue takes its orientation from Maurice Bévenot's groundbreaking research in the mid-1950s.[26] The argument is that the first version of *On the Unity of the Church* was written during the controversy with Novatian over the lapsed. In that version Cyprian argued for the supremacy of the Roman bishop in order to get Novatian to submit to the catholic church, unified under a hierarchical structure of bishops in which one bishop held primacy. Several years later the target of Cyprian's pen was Stephen, the bishop of Rome, and so it was no longer advantageous for Cyprian to champion the supremacy of Stephen's seat. Cyprian rewrote sections 4-5 in order to argue that each bishop was an heir of Peter and shared equal rank. Stuart Hall has recently called into question Bévenot's theory. In Hall's reading, version A is directed at Fortunatus and Felicissimus and version B has Novatian in mind.[27] Now, regardless of the precise circumstances that occasioned version A and the revision of version B (that is, whether Bévenot or Stuart is correct), the supremacy of the Roman bishop cannot be established from Cyprian's writings.[28] Either Cyprian retracted his earlier claim of Rome's supremacy (Bévenot) or neither version gave Rome the authority that the later church claimed it did (Stuart).

---

26 Maurice Bévenot, '"Primus Petro Datur": St. Cyprian on the Papacy,' *Journal of Theological Studies* n.s. 5 (1954): 19-35.

27 Stuart G. Hall, 'The Versions of Cyprian *De Unitate*, 4-5: Bévenot's Dating Revisited,' *Journal of Theological Studies* n.s. 55 (2004): 144-45.

28 Hall, 'The Versions of Cyprian,' 138. Hall states that neither version 'is 'papalist' in terms of either the medieval Conciliarist disputes or in terms of modern papalist and episcopalist arguments. Few have ventured the theory that version A (the Primacy Text) is the only authentic text. See J. Ludwig, 'Die Primatworte Mt. 16.18-19 in der altkirchlichen Exegese,' *Neutestamentliche Abhandlungen* 19 (1952): 20-36.

Cyprian did not give *carte blanche* to the Roman bishop, because each bishop played an essential role in his comprehensive understanding of the church. Every bishop shared the authority given to Peter. For this reason, a right view of bishops was necessary.

Bishops

The Roman society in which Cyprian was reared had a longstanding hierarchical structure. The top of the pecking order, of course, was the emperor, followed by the senatorial class (300 families), the equestrians (.01%), the decurions (5%), and then the rest of the populace in descending order of rank.[29] It was a society in which there was a large disparity between the wealthy and the poor, where the rich made up only five or six percent of the entire Empire. Although the Rome Empire was known for its social mobility, the vast majority of people died in the same class into which they were born. Most people lived a hand-to-mouth existence, simply trying to survive from one day to the next. One significant way that the wealthy helped the poor was through patron-client relationships.

A patron was a person of wealth and status who entered into a reciprocal relationship with a client from the poorer class. Each day the client would come to the patron's house to offer whatever services might be needed. It could range from housework to accompanying the patron as he strolled through the marketplace, because the more clients a patron had in tow, the greater his prestige. Reciprocally, a patron would provide for the needs of his clients be it healthcare or the need for a lawyer. The patron-client relationship was one of mutual benefit and necessary for the economic structure of Roman society.

In the broadest sense, the emperor thought of himself as a patron and all of his citizens as his clients. This funneled down

---

[29] See James S. Jeffers, *The Greco-Roman World of the New Testament Era: Exploring the Background of Early Christianity* (Downer's Grove: IVP Academic, 1999), p. 181.

to governors who viewed their provinces this way and down even further to local officials. Because of Cyprian's social standing prior to his conversion, he would have functioned as a patron in Carthage and would have had a number of clients at his beck and call. He even confessed to Donatus, 'The man who is attended by *crowds of clients*, and dignified by the numerous association of an officious train, regards it as a punishment when he is alone.'[30] Cyprian thought that becoming a Christian would mean to give up his train of clients, which he did for a season. However, after he became a bishop, he transformed this Roman model for the church, where now the bishop was the patron and the congregation was the client.[31] Once more, Cyprian had his throng of clients.[32]

We have already seen Cyprian's first move as a wealthy patron of the church when he donated his money and possessions to the church upon his conversion.[33] Brent believes Pontius

---

30 Cyprian, *Letter to Donatus* 3, emphasis added.

31 Already in the New Testament the apostle Paul was calling into question those Christians who would take advantage of a generous patron. This may be the background of Paul's comment in 2 Thessalonians 3:10, 'if anyone is not willing to work, let him not eat.' Bruce Winter observes, 'Paul would not endorse a Christian continuing as the recipient of private benefactions by way of a parasitic client relationship with a patron even though it was widely accepted in the secular world as an important element in the social fabric of public life' (*Seek the Welfare of the City* [Grand Rapids: Eerdmans, 1994], p. 42). Paul may in fact have been discouraging the rise of Christian patrons in the church. Whatever the case may be, by the time Cyprian became bishop in Carthage, he interpreted his role as the patron of the church and of the city.

32 Peter Brown speaks of the *clientele* who flocked to Cyprian (*The Making of Late Antiquity* [Cambridge, MA: Harvard University Press, 1978], p. 79).

33 Pontius, *The Life and Passion of Cyprian* 15. For a full treatment on Cyprian's view of himself as a patron, see Charles A. Bobertz's unpublished dissertation, 'Cyprian of Carthage as Patron: A Social and Historical Study of the Role of Bishop in the Ancient Christian Community of North Africa' (Ph.D. diss. Yale University, 1988). Bobertz takes a rather cynical view of Cyprian the patron, as though Cyprian just wanted to control the purse strings. Contrary to Bobertz's claim, Geoffrey Dunn suggests that Cyprian wished to 'turn his back on patronage' but found that appealing to patron-client relationships was the only way to get the rich Christians in Carthage to support the poor ('The White Crown of Works: Cyprian's Early Pastoral Ministry of Almsgiving in Carthage,' *Church History* 73.4 [2004]: 717–18).

shaped the story the way he did to show Cyprian as a patron.[34] By donating such a large sum of money, he became the *de facto* patron of the Carthaginian church, which meant that part of the congregation's responsibility to their patron would have meant voting him in at elections, the very thing they did by acclaiming him as their bishop.[35]

Viewing the bishop as a patron meant that the bishop had several important roles. First, he was a shepherd who provided food for his sheep, both literally and metaphorically, through dispensing food and preaching the Word. Second, the bishop was an administrator. As the church grew the role of bishop as administrator would have become a heavy burden. The word bishop itself is derived from the word *episkopos*, from which we derive episcopal, which had the idea of 'looking over' or 'visiting.'[36] He was tasked with looking over the affairs of the church just as a secular official would. Third, the bishop was the protector of orthodoxy. Even though the first ecumenical council would come nearly seventy-five years after Cyprian's death, there were many local councils that took place throughout the empire. A cluster of bishops within a certain geographic area would convene in order to handle matters of doctrine and practice. Cyprian gives grounding for these various roles in his letter to Lucius, the bishop of Rome: 'so the shepherd might be restored to feed his flock, and the pilot to manage the ship, and the ruler to govern the people.'[37]

Whatever one's view on church polity, it would seem that the episcopacy was important for the early church both to keep her unified and to protect her from doctrinal error. Bishops were the gatekeepers of sacred truth. This is why Ignatius said things like,

---

34 Brent, *Cyprian and Roman Carthage*, 72.

35 Brent, *Cyprian and Roman Carthage*, 72.

36 LSJ, s.v. *episkopos*.

37 Cyprian, *Letter* 57.1. Hall notes that even 'shepherding . . . in ancient times . . . signifie[d] government and punishment' ('The Versions of Cyprian,' 142-43).

'Do nothing without the bishop,'[38] and why Irenaeus hung much of his argument for catholicity on apostolic succession through the bishops.[39] Cyprian acknowledged this idea of apostolic succession speaking of bishops 'who by vicarious ordination succeed to the apostles.'[40] When even the slightest whiff of error was detected in the shifting winds of heresy, the bishops would coalesce to give a response. Truly for Cyprian, the 'glory of the bishop is the glory of the church'[41] who is 'chosen by divine appointment.'[42]

J. Patout Burns summarized Cyprian's tenure as a bishop in this way: 'Three questions dominated his episcopate: the unity and unicity of the church, the purity of the church, and the efficacy of the church's ritual actions.'[43] These three streams converged in the bishop, whose responsibility it was to keep the church united and pure and to demonstrate these qualities of the church through the sacraments.

The sacraments — baptism and Eucharist

Cyprian's dominant concern for unity undergirded his view of the sacraments, which he made clear in the controversy over rebaptism. Fundamentally that controversy was over the unity of the church and the inability of those outside the church to practice Christian baptism. The Eucharist also symbolized Christian unity, as can be seen in the elements themselves.

---

38 Ignatius, *Magnesians* 7.1, trans. Michael Holmes, *The Apostolic Fathers*, 3rd ed. (Grand Rapids: Baker Academic, 2007), p. 207.

39 Irenaeus, *Against Heresies* 3.3. Maurice Wiles makes the interesting point that Cyprian flips Irenaeus's argument. 'So far from the succession of bishops being grounded upon the succession of the Church, it is the other way round; the succession of the Church is grounded upon and constituted by the succession of bishops' ('The Theological Legacy of St. Cyprian,' in *Journal of Ecclesiastical History* 14 [1963]: 144).

40 Cyprian, *Letter* 68.4.

41 Cyprian, *Letter* 6.1.

42 Cyprian, *Letter* 57.3.

43 J. Patout Burns, 'Cyprian of Carthage,' *Expository Times* 120 (2009): 471.

Cyprian pressed allegory into his service to make the clever argument that a single loaf of bread contains many grains and a single bottle of wine is composed of a cluster of grapes, indicating the Church's unity.[44] Thus, whether it is around the baptismal font or the table, the church professes her oneness in Christ through the sacraments. As a bishop it was his duty to protect and administer these grace-filled symbols of the faith.

A word on Cyprian's use of 'sacrament' is needful before moving forward. The word sacrament itself comes from the Roman military idea of oath taking. A soldier demonstrated his allegiance by taking an oath, which was his *sacramentum*. Cyprian freely uses the word *sacramentum*, which has a threefold meaning in Cyprian: 'the confession of faith as an oath binding one to Christ, the whole of the divine mystery, and the rites that signify this mystery.'[45] For the purposes of this section, it is the third definition that is important. Sacraments were more than just ordinances to be observed in obedience to Scripture; they are religious rites that symbolize divine mystery. The sacraments were central to worship and salvation, leading him to say we should 'keep the way of life through the saving sacraments.'[46] Cyprian made substantial contributions to the church's understanding of baptism and the Eucharist.[47]

In *Letter* 73, written to Pompey against Stephen, Cyprian laid out all the things that happen in baptism. The baptized are renewed and sanctified, freed from the devil, filled with the Holy Spirit, able to put away their sins, spiritually reformed into new people, partakers of the second birth, and receivers of salvation.[48] The presence of the Spirit in baptism was critical.

---

44 Cyprian, *Letter* 75.6. cf. Cyprian, *Letter* 62.13 and *Didache* 9.4.

45 See Everett Ferguson, *Baptism in the Early Church: History, Theology, and Liturgy in the First Five Centuries* (Grand Rapids: Eerdmans, 2009), p. 360.

46 Cyprian, *Three Books Against the Jews*, preface.

47 Cyprian also made inroads into the sacrament of penance, which received treatment in the last chapter and will be discussed more in the following chapter.

48 Cyprian, *Letter* 73.5, 11, 16. See Everett Ferguson, *Baptism in the Early Church*, pp. 357–59.

Water cannot wash away sins without the Spirit.[49] And Cyprian is clear that faith is necessary to acquire the Spirit.[50] Therefore, baptism must be accompanied by faith and the Spirit for the individual to receive salvation.

Cyprian was baptized as a mature adult, probably in his forties. As he reflected on his baptism, and the nature of baptism itself, he wrote, 'We had renounced the world when we were baptized; but we have now indeed renounced the world when tried and approved by God, we leave all that we have, and have followed the Lord, and stand and live in His faith and fear.'[51] Baptism marks the separation of the individual from the world—the definitive moment of discipleship when sins are remitted[52] and the Holy Spirit comes upon the believer through the laying on of hands by the bishop, who would seal the baptizand with the sign of the cross on the forehead.[53]

According to Everett Ferguson's landmark work *Baptism in the Early Church*, Cyprian faced three controversies regarding baptism: rebaptism for those baptized by heretics or schismatics, clinical or sickbed baptism, and infant baptism.[54] The first we

---

49 Cyprian, *Letter* 73.5.

50 Cyprian, *Letter* 75.12.

51 Cyprian, *Letter* 6.5.

52 Cyprian unequivocally stated, 'In baptism remission of sins is granted once for all' (*On Works and Alms*, 2).

53 Cyprian, *Letters* 73.5; 72.9. For the sign of the cross, which he makes with reference to Ezek 9:4–6, Exod 12:13, and Rev 14:1, see *To Demetrianus* 22. See Ferguson, *Baptism in the Early Church*, p. 355.

54 Ferguson, *Baptism in the Early Church*, 351. I am in Ferguson's debt in this section on baptism. His is the best work on baptism in the patristic era. For other significant work, see G. W. H. Lampe, *The Seal and the Spirit: A Study in the Doctrine of Baptism and Confirmation in the New Testament and the Fathers* (London: SPCK, 1967), and David Wright, 'The Origins of Infant Baptism—Child Believers' Baptism?' *Scottish Journal of Theology* 39 (1987): 1–23. Of course there is the classic debate between J. Jeremias, *Infant Baptism in the First Four Centuries* (Philadelphia: Westminster, 1960) and Kurt Aland, *Did the Early Christian Church Baptize Infants?*, trans. G. R. Beasley-Murray (London: SCM Press, 1963). See Ferguson, *Baptism in the Early Church*, 362n.1 for a stout list of resources on the issue of infant baptism in the Fathers, which demonstrates the vast amount of attention this topic has received.

have touched on already. The problem pertaining to sickbed baptism is that many people postponed baptism until they neared death so that they would not be guilty of post-baptismal sins.[55] By the time they were too sick to receive baptism by immersion (*lavacri*—washing), the only option was sprinkling (*aspargi*).[56] There were some who opposed this practice, but Cyprian defended it because the point is what takes place in baptism and not the mode. But he was not dogmatic about this— each person should judge what he thinks is right.[57]

One of Cyprian's enduring contributions to the church was his argument for infant baptism. Few things have garnered more attention, or more intense debate, in early Christian studies than this topic. Tertullian is one of the first to mention the practice but only to disagree. He seems to think that it goes against tradition. He encouraged, 'Let them become Christians when they have become able to know Christ,' and that, as long as death or sickness did not loom, a 'delay of baptism is preferable... in the case of little children.'[58] Tradition soon gave way to practicality in a society with a high infant mortality rate, and exegetical grounding was needed. Ferguson has astutely commented, 'As has often been true in Christian history, the practice preceded its doctrinal defense.'[59] Cyprian and Origen were the first to provide a biblical basis for the practice of infant baptism.[60]

---

55 Tertullian, for example, allowed for only one sin after baptism, which would have encouraged people to delay baptism as long as possible. This practice of delaying baptism became even more common in the fourth century, most notably by Constantine.

56 Ferguson, *Baptism in the Early Church*, 355. Cyprian rummaged through the Old Testament to find references to sprinkling, using Ezek 36:25-26 and Num 8:5-7, 19:8, 12, 13, 19 as proof texts (Cyprian, *Letter* 75.12).

57 Cyprian, *Letter* 75.12.

58 Tertullian, *On Baptism* 18.

59 Ferguson, *Baptism in the Early Church*, p. 369.

60 We have space here only to discuss Cyprian's view. For Origen's contribution to the discussion, see Ferguson, *Baptism in the Early Church*, p. 367-70.

Cyprian's case for infant baptism largely comes from *Letter* 58, which he wrote to Fidus about a synod held in Africa in 252 or 253. Fidus argued that baptism should come on the eighth day in the same way that circumcision was performed by the Jews. Cyprian and the other sixty-six bishops unanimously rejected the idea that baptism was circumcision reconstituted. Circumcision was a sacrament given to the Jews 'in shadow and in usage.'[61] Infants should, however, be baptized on the eighth day, but because Jesus rose from the dead on the eighth day, not in keeping with the outmoded practice of circumcision.[62] Cyprian is happy to speak of baptism as 'circumcision of the spirit' and 'spiritual circumcision' but not as a figure of 'carnal circumcision' which ceased when Christ came.[63]

The challenge for second- and third-century fathers was reconciling infant baptism and infant innocence. Infant baptism was practiced but the reasons were not yet clear. Infants had not committed sins so why did they need baptism for the remission of sins? The text driving infant baptism was John 3:5: 'Truly, truly I say to you, unless one is born of water and the Spirit, he cannot enter the kingdom of God.' Water in this verse was universally understood as baptism, thus making entrance into heaven contingent on baptism. Cyprian reasons that if we would not keep the vilest of sinners who repented and believed from being baptized, then,

> . . . how much rather ought we to shrink from hindering an infant, who, being lately born, has not sinned, except in that, being born after the flesh according to Adam, he has contracted the contagion of the ancient death at its earliest birth, who approaches the more easily on this very account to the reception of the forgiveness of sins—that to him are remitted, not his own sins, but the sins of another?[64]

---

61 Cyprian, *Letter* 58.4.

62 Cyprian says this despite the fact that Fidus's critique was that churches were baptizing babies on the second or third day of life (*Letter* 58.2).

63 Cyprian, *Letter* 58.4.

64 Cyprian, *Letter* 58.5.

Prohibiting children from coming to the fount of everlasting life is age discrimination. In a pre-Jeffersonian statement, Cyprian declares, 'all men are like and equal, since they have once been made by God; and our age may have a difference in the increase of our bodies, according to the world, but not according to God.'[65] Every person bears Adam's contagion and we sin against the youngest if we refuse them the laver that will wash away the stain of Adam's transgression.[66] Ferguson cautions against reading too much of a connection between Adam's sin and the need for baptism, arguing that the church would have to wait for Augustine to make the connection between infant baptism and original sin.[67] However, it is difficult to deny that Cyprian does not have an early version of the doctrine of original sin here. Because infants can suffer death, and because they have Adam's contagion in some sense, they need to be given the grace of baptism in order to attain eternal life. To bar infants from baptism is to hinder them from God's mercy.[68]

Another reason to baptize infants is that it provides the grace they need for all of life. All the profits of baptism listed above become the child's via the faith of the sponsor. He confirms this by recounting an anecdote of a baptized infant whose parents rushed off to make a sacrifice during the persecution.[69] The child was given bread dipped in wine that had been part of a sacrificial offering. When the child returned to church with her parents she was restless during prayer and would alternate between weeping and tossing about uncontrollably. At the point of the 'sacrifice' (the Eucharist), the deacon offered the cup to those present and

---

65 Cyprian, *Letter* 58.3.

66 Note that Cyprian argues that the infant 'has not sinned.'

67 Ferguson, *Baptism in the Early Church*, 371. Though, interestingly enough, Augustine argues from infant baptism to original sin, instead of from original sin to baptism. The practice initially dictated the doctrine. Eventually the doctrine of original sin was constructed in its own right.

68 Cyprian, *Letter* 58.6.

69 For this story, see Cyprian, *On the Lapsed* 25.

the child, 'by the instinct of divine majesty, turned away its face, compressed its mouth with resisting lips, and refused the cup.'[70] The deacon persisted and forced the elements into the child's mouth, which caused the little girl to vomit. Cyprian concluded, 'in a profane body and mouth the Eucharist could not remain.'[71] This baptized child was unwittingly forced into idolatry, so the Spirit made her reject the Eucharist in order to protect herself.

Children are every bit as able to receive spiritual things as adults. They need baptism early because the spiritual forces of evil will not spare them in their youth. This marks a point of departure for Cyprian from Tertullian. Steven McKinion summarizes the difference between the two Carthaginians: 'For Tertullian, baptism was administered to a believer who had repented of past sins; for Cyprian, it could also be administered to an infant who would need its benefits for a future Christian life.'[72]

From early on baptism was a prerequisite to the other major sacrament Cyprian wrote about, the Eucharist.[73] Baptism was the single act in which sins are remitted and the Spirit is received, but the Eucharist should be received daily as 'the food of salvation.'[74] The Eucharist, taken from the Greek *eucharisteō*, meaning 'to give thanks,' was the centerpiece of early Christian worship.[75] Ignatius called it the 'medicine of immortality' (*pharmakon athanasias*)[76] and Justin Martyr said the Eucharist is not 'common bread and common drink.'[77]

---

70 This is a striking example of paedo-communion in the early church.
71 Cyprian, *On the Lapsed* 25.
72 Steven A. McKinion, 'Baptism in the Patristic Writings,' in *Believer's Baptism: Sign of the New Covenant in Christ*, ed. Thomas R. Schreiner and Shawn D. Wright (NAC Studies in Bible & Theology; Nashville: B&H Academic, 2006), p. 179.
73 Cyprian, *Letter* 62.8. Cf. Justin Martyr, *1 Apology* 66.
74 Cyprian, *On the Lord's Prayer* 18.
75 The first reference to the Lord's Supper as the Eucharist is found in the *Didache* 9.1-4.
76 See Ignatius, *Ephesians* 20.2.
77 Justin Martyr, *1 Apology* 66.

Cyprian gave the first extended explanation of the Eucharist in the ante-Nicene church,[78] specifically aimed at the error of an aquarian Eucharist, that is, using water instead of wine in the Supper, because 'the blood of Christ is assuredly not water, but wine.'[79] Tradition and symbolism require that the fruit of the vine is crushed and drunk. Yet the cup is not only wine—it is wine mingled with water. Water was not used to cut the wine's potency; it was used to picture Christ's passion more closely (blood *and* water flowed from Jesus' side [John 19:34]), and to symbolize the relationship between Christ and His people.[80]

In *Letter* 62 Cyprian addressed the problem of a water only Eucharist by setting forth the tradition that came from the Old Testament and Christ Himself. Wine in the Supper was foreshadowed by types in the Old Testament. Noah was drunk on wine and not water (Gen 9:21), Melchizedek set out bread and wine (Gen 14:18), Solomon spoke of the bread and mingled wine (Prov 9:5), Judah prophesied of Christ that His garment would be washed in the blood of the grape (Gen 49:11), and Isaiah likewise spoke of red garments from the wine-press (Isa 63:3). Cyprian takes advantage of the wine press image because in order to make wine, grapes must be trodden and pressed, just like Jesus had to be trodden and pressed in His suffering. He first drank of the cup that He gives His followers to drink.[81]

Wine is necessary not only for its rich symbolism, but because wine has the power to intoxicate. The Holy Spirit wrote

---

[78] The first full-length treatment on the Lord's Supper did not come until the ninth-century when Paschasius Radbertus (d *c.* 860) wrote *On the Body and Blood of the Lord*. A very helpful introduction to the Lord's Supper in the Fathers can be found in Michael A. G. Haykin, '"A Glorious Inebriation": Eucharistic Thought and Piety in the Patristic Era,' in *The Lord's Supper: Remembering and Proclaiming Christ until He Comes*, ed. Thomas R. Schreiner and Matthew R. Crawford (NAC Studies in Bible & Theology; Nashville: B&H Academic, 2010), pp. 103-26.

[79] Cyprian, *Letter* 62.2.

[80] Cyprian, *Letter* 62.5. cf. John 19:34.

[81] Cyprian, *Letter* 62.7.

of the intoxicating cup in Psalm 23:5. Cyprian's version of the Old Latin (Ps 22:5) read, 'Your inebriating cup, how excellent it is!' (*calix tuus inebrians perquam optimus*). The overflowing cup of the Hebrew text was translated and interpreted in the Greek and Latin texts to discuss the quality of the drink more than the quantity. The cup overflows with inebriation, bringing cheer, something water cannot do. What makes the Lord's cup so powerful is that its intoxicating wine leads to sobriety. With majestic imagery Cyprian writes,

> Doubtless the Lord's cup so inebriates them that drink, that it makes them sober; that it restores their minds to spiritual wisdom; that each one recovers from the flavor of the world to the understanding of God; and in the same way, that by that common wine the mind is dissolved, and the soul relaxed, and all sadness is laid aside, so, when the blood of the Lord and the cup of salvation have been drunk, the memory of the old man is laid aside, and there arises an oblivion of the former worldly conversation, and the sorrowful and sad breast which before was oppressed by tormenting sins is eased by the joy of divine mercy.

The irony is thick. Wine that leads to drunkenness is transformed in the Eucharist to produce sobriety. The drink that usually clouds the mind instead restores wisdom; the cup that brought worldliness now brings godliness; the sorrow of debauchery is changed into the joy of mercy. Cyprian's vision of the Eucharist is missing from many evangelical traditions. The cup should inebriate us with a sense of God that makes us forget the world and care only for the things of heaven.[82] This, indeed, is sobriety!

The Eucharist has many other spiritual benefits. The Eucharist arms believers against the adversary.[83] There is power in the blood to ward off Satan and the temptations that daily

---

82 Cyprian, *Letter* 62.11.

83 Cyprian, *Letter* 53.2.

infiltrate the heart.[84] The Eucharist also provides courage for the Christian life, such that we might shed our blood as we remember Him who shed His blood for us. Only those who have drank from the cup of the Lord will be fit to drink from the cup of martyrdom.[85]

Having argued for the necessity of wine, Cyprian builds a case for the use of water as well. The Eucharist is invalidated when water is used without wine just as it is when wine is used without water. In keeping with his overarching doctrine of unity, Cyprian connects the water and wine to believers and Christ, respectively. When the water is mixed with the wine, it symbolizes Christ's union with His people. Both elements must be mixed in the cup for the Eucharist to be present. 'For if any one offer wine only, the blood of Christ is dissociated from us; but if the water be alone, the people are dissociated from Christ.'[86] Thus, the Eucharist is a sacrament of sober intoxication where the church celebrates her redemption and unity, which in turn empowers believers to live for God.

The Eucharist was much more than just a moment of sober intoxication in Cyprian's thinking—it was a sacrifice. He indicates that the bishop, or presiding minister (often called a president), offers a 'full sacrifice' in the way that Christ offered Himself as a sacrifice,[87] and even says, 'because we make mention of His passion in all *sacrifices* (for the Lord's passion is the sacrifice we offer), we ought to do nothing else than what He did.'[88] Along

---

[84] Cyprian, *On the Lord's Prayer* 18. Cyprian interprets Jesus' connection, 'Give us this day our daily bread' to 'forgive us our trespasses' as our need for the Eucharist daily. See below on Cyprian's reading of the Lord's Prayer.

[85] Cyprian, *Letter* 53.2.

[86] Cyprian, *Letter* 62.13.

[87] Cyprian, *Letter* 62.14.

[88] Cyprian, *Letter* 62.17. The argument Cyprian used against an aquarian Eucharist is that Jesus did not use water only. Likewise, the reason to conceive of the Eucharist as a sacrifice is to imitate the actual sacrifice of Christ (see Paul F. Bradshaw, *Eucharistic Origins* [Eugene, OR: Wipf & Stock, 2012], p. 110). Cyprian makes this connection to imitation especially in *Letter* 62.14.

with Cyprian calling the Supper a sacrifice was his frequent use of the title priest (*sacerdos*), who was tasked with offering the sacrifices of the Eucharist.[89] Cyprian may not have been first to use this word, but he does seem to normalize it in early Christian vocabulary.

Scholars divide over Cyprian's language of sacrifice, some suggesting that he is arguing for real presence, while others think the language should not be pressed so hard. Those who perceive Cyprian to be speaking figuratively think that he was communicating that just as Jesus died on the cross, so now the priest offers the sacrifice in memory of Him.[90] Others, though, think he is communicating some version of real presence, which has credence given his usage of the terms priest and sacrifice. Mayes, who sees some form of real presence in the Supper, comments, 'For Cyprian, there was no separation of Christ's blood and consecrated wine. The wine is the blood of Jesus and vice versa.'[91] The substance used to fill the cup mattered to Cyprian because it must accurately reflect the blood of Christ. He argued, 'the blood of Christ is not offered if there be no wine in the cup, nor the Lord's sacrifice celebrated with a legitimate consecration unless our oblation and sacrifice respond to His passion.'[92] Although Cyprian does appear to have in mind some level of real presence, we must not think that Cyprian

---

89 For the development of priestly language, see Paul F. Bradshaw, *The Search for the Origins of Christian Worship: Sources and Methods for the Study of Early Liturgy*, 2nd ed. (Oxford: Oxford University Press, 2002), 201-05. Robert J. H. Mayes is probably right to suggest that 'the plural "sacrifices" is used because Cyprian as a bishop had oversight over many congregations where the Sacrament was celebrated, as opposed to just one "sacrifice" at one altar' ('The Lord's Supper in the Theology of Cyprian of Carthage,' *Concordia Theological Quarterly* 74 [2010]: 314).

90 See John D. Laurance, *'Priest' as Type of Christ: The Leader of the Eucharist in Salvation History according to Cyprian of Carthage* (New York: Peter Lang, 1984). See also Ernest Bartels who believed that the Supper was only symbolic in Cyprian's view (*Take Eat, Take Drink: The Lord's Supper through the Centuries* [St. Louis: Concordia Publishing House, 2004]: 80).

91 Mayes, 'The Lord's Supper in the Theology of Cyprian of Carthage,' 307-324.

92 Cyprian, *Letter* 62.9.

had developed a view of transubstantiation like that in the Middle Ages. Cyprian is an important link in the chain that would eventually lead to a doctrine of transubstantiation, but his thoughts were not nearly developed enough on this.

As far as the sacraments are concerned, baptism and the Eucharist are the twin pillars upon which virtue is built. Baptism seals us in Christ and initiates our course of piety; the Eucharist provides weekly nourishment in the faith. The road to Christian maturity begins here, but Cyprian had much more advice to give about how to live as Christians.

4

CYPRIAN AND THE CHRISTIAN LIFE

Peter Hinchliff summarized the typical portrait of Cyprian when he asserted, 'The story of Cyprian's life is the story of how the cold disciplinarian became the hero of Christian Carthage.'[1] To be sure, Cyprian can come across as a 'cold disciplinarian,' rigid and uncompromising, harsh and dictatorial, but this is only because we read him in the middle of controversy. The few non-polemical writings available show a different side of the bishop, a side of piety and grace, compassion and love. We must not let Cyprian the strong-willed leader overshadow Cyprian the tender-hearted shepherd, who possessed deep spirituality, from the intensity of his prayers to his spiritual view of suffering, death, and martyrdom. To overlook Cyprian's spirituality is a grave mistake that is too often made, leaving the wrong impression of his life, ministry, and death.

The only description we have of his physical countenance comes from Pontius, who provides a brief description of Cyprian that is tinged with hagiography. Yet in this sketch we catch a glimmer of his virtue.

---

1   Peter Hinchliff, *Cyprian of Carthage and the Unity of the Christian Church* (London: Geoffrey Chapman, 1974), p. 4.

> So much sanctity and grace beamed from his face that it confounded the minds of the beholders. His countenance was grave and joyous. Neither was his severity gloomy, nor his affability excessive, but a mingled tempering of both; so that it might be doubted whether he most deserved to be revered or to be loved, except that he deserved both to be revered and to be loved. And his dress was not out of harmony with his countenance, being itself also subdued to a fitting mean. The pride of the world did not inflame him.[2]

Again we see that Cyprian laid aside worldly rank and dress for the humble life of a Christian bishop. For Pontius, Cyprian embodied a pleasant mixture of austerity and affability, making him a perfect candidate for the episcopacy. Cyprian was resolute and uncompromising when truth and order were on the line, but he could be kind and compassionate in caring for the individual soul.

Cyprian's piety will be divided into three main sections in this chapter. First, we will listen in on the bishop in prayer. The main focus will be Cyprian's treatise *On the Lord's Prayer*, though prayer is laced all throughout his other writings. It was commonplace for patristic authors to punctuate their writings with prayer and praise mid paragraph, much like Paul would stop and offer doxological statements when the weight of the truth he just explained was too heavy not to pause and lift his voice in exaltation. (Regrettably, we have lost this feature of discourse in modern writing in a vain attempt at neutrality.) Second, we will trace the theme of virtue through Cyprian's writings. Finally, we will discover how Cyprian's understanding of suffering, martyrdom, and death shaped his outlook on the Christian life.

Prayer — 'Matters of deep moment'

Within the span of a ten-year episcopate, Cyprian encountered two persecutions, a plague, and several mutinies in his church.

---

2 Pontius, *The Life and Passion of Cyprian* 6.

What got him through this decade that was dense with trials was a life saturated in prayer. Cyprian was committed to stoking the flame of his spirituality with the hot iron of continual prayer to God. He sought to live *coram Deo*, which is an expression the Fathers used to speak of living in the presence of God. All of life should be purposefully lived as though God was in the room, as he reminds his reader, 'Let us consider that we are standing in God's sight.'[3] If God's presence was felt to this degree, then it naturally led to a vivid life of prayer, and this was true for Cyprian.

Prayer should be based on Scripture. In order for prayer to be centered on God's own words, there must be a back and forth between pouring ourselves out in prayer and filling ourselves up with Scripture. 'Be constant as well in prayer as in reading; now speak with God, now let God speak with you, let Him instruct you in His precepts, let Him direct you.'[4] The person who prays Scripture will not only always pray truth, but he will also be led by God into his precepts.

If Scripture is the melody of prayer, then the heart is the instrument. Cyprian appeals to Hannah as one who prayed from the heart. 'Hannah. . . who was a type of the Church. . . in that she prayed to God not with clamorous petition, but silently and modestly, within the very recesses of her heart. She spoke with hidden prayer, but with manifest faith. She spoke not with her voice, but with her heart, because she knew that thus God hears.'[5] It is to the innermost part of the heart that a person must retreat if she is to experience a depth of communion with God, for it is in the heart that our true selves can be found, far away from the distractions of life and the praises of man. Following the words of Jesus, Cyprian encourages private prayer that God alone will hear, because God

---

3 Cyprian, *On the Lord's Prayer* 4.

4 Cyprian, *To Donatus* 15.

5 Cyprian, *On the Lord's Prayer* 5.

hears faith not sound. The person that comes to God with modest fear and manifest faith can trust that he will be heard.

While God listens to the heart and while private prayer is important, indeed vital, prayer should primarily be a communal event. 'The teacher of peace and the Master of unity would not have prayer to be made singly and individually, as for one who prays to pray for himself alone... Our prayer is public and common; and when we pray, we pray not for one, but for the whole people, because we the whole people are one.'[6] Since the church is unified, prayer must be performed in community in order to signify that the people are united. It is unsurprising that Cyprian desires to see the church united in prayer since unity was at the center of his theology. Prayer in community is a symphony unto God, where the many voices blend into one powerful, sonorous voice. When prayer is not conducted in one accord, treacherous things can happen. Reflecting on the factions that had threatened the church, Cyprian told his clergy, 'these evils would not have come upon the brethren, if the brotherhood had been animated with one spirit,'[7] and had 'they continued with one accord in prayer, declaring both by the urgency and by the agreement of their praying, that God, who makes men to dwell of one mind in a house, only admits into the divine and eternal home those among whom prayer is unanimous,'[8] then the church would not have been fractured.

One word that surfaces frequently when Cyprian speaks of prayer is 'urgent.' Prayer was urgent for Cyprian, something that must be sought with earnestness, tears, and groaning. If Jesus said we should knock, then let us beat on heaven's door until God hears and responds. 'Let us ask, and we shall receive; and if there by delay and tardiness in our receiving, since we have grievously offended, let us knock, because to him that knocks

---

6 Cyprian, *On the Lord's Prayer* 8.

7 Cyprian, *Letter* 7.3.

8 Cyprian, *On the Lord's Prayer* 8.

also it shall be opened, if only prayers, our groaning, and our tears, knock at the door; and with these we must be urgent and persevering, even though prayer be offered with one mind.'[9] And again, 'Let us urgently pray and groan with continual petitions. . . . Let us therefore strike off and break away from the bonds of sleep, and pray with urgency and watchfulness.'[10] Cyprian knew the human tendency for slothfulness in prayer. Just as the apostles slept when they should have been vigilantly praying, we too must stay awake and watchful and recognize that we will only be successful in prayer if we pursue it urgently. But prayer alone is not always enough. Certain times demand that God's people seek Him in prayer and fasting. Cyprian writes, 'in order to appease and entreat the Lord, we must lament not only in words, but also with fastings and with tears, and with every kind of urgency.'[11] Fasting adds a layer of desperation to the request, ensuring that we not only plead with words, but we demonstrate our hunger for God by abstaining from food.[12]

Cyprian knew that speaking of the importance of prayer, or even speaking often about prayer, does not instruct a person on how to pray. Fledgling believers are left in the nest if they are simply told to pray but are never shown how to soar to the heavens. The disciples once asked Jesus how they should pray and He gave to them what we call the Lord's Prayer. In the midst of the controversies that demanded his immediate attention, Cyprian found time to write the brief work *On the Lord's Prayer*

---

9 Cyprian, *Letter* 7.2. Part of the urgency comes with the occasion of this letter. Cyprian references the Decian persecution and those who have done evil by sowing seeds of discord among the brethren. Cyprian wanted to stir up the clergy in Carthage to seek the face of God in prayer, for the hour of trial was upon them.

10 Cyprian, *Letter* 7.5.

11 Cyprian, *Letter* 7.1.

12 Towards the end of the treatise, Cyprian quotes Tobit 12:8 which says, 'Prayer is good with fasting and almsgiving.' Cyprian uses this to say that we should not offer 'fruitless or naked prayers,' meaning that we should not come to God with words alone, but should demonstrate our earnestness with fasting and almsgiving. See Cyprian, *On the Lord's Prayer* 32.

(*De Dominica Oratione*), probably written in 252 in the aftermath of the Decian persecution, in order to instruct people on how to pray.[13] This verse-by-verse exposition of the Lord's Prayer became the standard work on prayer in the early church, at least in the west, so much so that when Hilary of Poitiers comes to the Lord's Prayer in his commentary on Matthew 6, he does not comment but instead sends his reader to Cyprian's masterpiece on prayer.[14] The Lord's Prayer is the template, or the paradigm, for prayer. 'For what can be a more spiritual prayer,' Cyprian asks, 'than that which was given to us by Christ, by whom also the Holy Spirit was given to us?'[15] Christ gave us the prayer and the Spirit by which to pray this prayer. He exhorts, 'Let Him also who dwells within our breast Himself dwell in our voice.'[16] Our words find the throne of God when the Spirit who lives inside us, inhabits the voice of our prayers. Prayer is nothing more than praying God's Word back to Him. 'It is a loving and friendly prayer to beseech God with His own word, to come up to His ear in the prayer of Christ.'[17] This will happen when we pray the words that Jesus taught us to pray. So assured was Cyprian that the Lord's Prayer is *the* model that he averred, 'to pray otherwise than He taught is not ignorance alone, but also sin.'[18]

Prayer is what brings depth to piety. Just before launching into his exposition of the Lord's Prayer, Cyprian exclaimed,

---

13 The Lord's Prayer was a key guide for prayer in the early church. Again, Cyprian is indebted to Tertullian, who also wrote a treatise on the Lord's Prayer, from which Cyprian clearly draws. Origen also wrote a treatise on the Lord's Prayer. For the Lord's Prayer in North Africa, see Michael Joseph Brown, *The Lord's Prayer through North African Eyes: A Window into Early Christianity* (New York: T & T Clark, 2004). For some reason Brown ends his discussion with Tertullian and offers up very little on Cyprian, even though Cyprian's work became the standard writing on the Lord's Prayer.

14 Gerard Joseph Ward, 'The Doctrine of Prayer in Third-Century Christian Africa' (M.A. thesis, University of Durham, 1981), p. 46.

15 Cyprian, *On the Lord's Prayer* 2.

16 Cyprian, *On the Lord's Prayer* 3.

17 Cyprian, *On the Lord's Prayer* 3.

18 Cyprian, *On the Lord's Prayer* 2.

'But what matters of deep moment are contained in the Lord's prayers!'[19] Prayer brings a depth of relationship that comes when God's people commune with Him through His appointed means of prayer. Shallowness of spirituality is nothing new. For those suffering from spiritual lethargy, Cyprian's first question would likely have been aimed at how much time a person spends with God in prayer. Those who want to descend into deeper places with God must let Jesus guide them with His own prayers.

Prayer begins with a recognition of sonship in the declaration, 'Our Father'. The new man who has been born again, can boldly approach God as a son, which would be blasphemy had Jesus not led us to do so.

> But how great is the Lord's indulgence! How great His condescension and plenteousness of goodness towards us, seeing that He has wished us to pray in the sight of God in such a way as to call God Father, and to call ourselves sons of God, even as Christ is the Son of God, a name which none of us would dare to venture on in prayer, unless He Himself had allowed us thus to pray![20]

To call God our Father is a privilege that places high demands on our lives. If He is our Father, then we must act as children of His holy name.

Being a child of God should not create in us overfamiliarity, however. The second clause of the prayer is, 'Hallowed be Your name.' God is a holy God and to pray in accord with His holiness, we should ask that He sanctify us as well. Our constant prayer should be sanctification, which is received by God's grace.[21] Next comes the request that God's kingdom come and that His will be done here on earth as it is in heaven. It is natural that a child of God who lives in pilgrimage on earth should aspire for things

---

19   Cyprian, *On the Lord's Prayer* 9.
20   Cyprian, *On the Lord's Prayer* 11.
21   Cyprian, *On the Lord's Prayer* 12.

to be done here as they are in His heavenly country, for 'he who dedicates himself to God and Christ desires not earthly, but heavenly kingdoms.'[22] In order to be a Christian, a person must choose a kingdom—he cannot straddle the line between the two.

Cyprian has a superb section under the heading of 'Your will be done, as in heaven so in earth,' that spells out his vision for what God's will looks like in the life of a believer.

> Now [this] is the will of God which Christ both did and taught. Humility in conversation; steadfastness in faith; modesty in words; justice in deeds; mercifulness in works; discipline in morals; to be unable to do a wrong, and to be able to bear a wrong when done; to keep peace with the brethren; to love God with all one's heart; to love Him in that He is a Father; to fear Him in that He is God; to prefer nothing whatever to Christ, because he did not prefer anything to us; to adhere inseparably to His love; to stand by His cross bravely and faithfully, when there is any contest on behalf of His name and honor, to exhibit in discourse that constancy wherewith we make confession; in torture, that confidence wherewith we do battle, in death, that patience whereby we are crowned—this is to desire to be fellow heirs with Christ; this is to do the commandment of God; this is to fulfill the will of the Father.[23]

It seems that most Christians reduce God's will for their life to who they should marry, what college they should attend, what career to pursue, how many white slats they need for their picket fence, and how little they need to give to keep their retirements cushy. Even worse, some seek God's will, or God's approval, for things that Scripture explicitly condemns. For Cyprian, to pray for God's will to be done is to pray that we might be transformed into the image of Christ. When Christians display the character of Christ in their lives, as listed above, they are fulfilling the will of God. Thus, we should not think of God's will as some

---

22 Cyprian, *On the Lord's Prayer* 13.

23 Cyprian, *On the Lord's Prayer* 15.

mystical thing that cannot be discerned; rather, God's will is becoming a certain type of person, which fueled Cyprian's ideas of virtue (to be discussed below). God's heavenly will becomes an earthly reality when Christians exhibit lives of humility, justice, peace, love, and the courage to fear God and not man or circumstance.

'Give us this day our daily bread,' should be understood literally and spiritually. Literally, we should recognize that God provides for our daily needs. Jesus taught us that we ought to renounce everything which places us in greater dependence on God. Spiritually, and of far greater importance, is the bread that is the body of Christ, who said 'I am the bread of life which came down from heaven. If any man eat of my bread, he shall live forever: and the bread which I will give is my flesh, for the life of the world' (John 6:51).[24] The Eucharist is given daily in the church so that believers might receive 'the food of salvation' and not be cut off from the heavenly bread.[25]

Also within the Lord's Prayer is a confession of sin and an acknowledgment of forgiveness—'forgive us our debts, as we also forgive our debtors.' According to Cyprian, no one could boast that he has overcome sin. 'Lest anyone should flatter himself that he is innocent, and by exalting himself should more deeply perish, he is instructed and taught that he sins daily.'[26] The reason we need the daily bread of Christ's body in the Eucharist is because we sin every day. Jesus intentionally placed the request for forgiveness after the request for food so that the one who sins would remember that there is provision for sin in partaking of the bread of life. With the plea for our forgiveness also comes the command to forgive others, which would have been exceptionally difficult for believers who were just coming out of

---

24 Cyprian, *On the Lord's Prayer* 18. This is Cyprian's version as he cites it in the text.

25 Cyprian, *On the Lord's Prayer* 18.

26 Cyprian, *On the Lord's Prayer* 22. On this point, one can see a clear line of departure from Tertullian and his rigorism. Cyprian acknowledged daily sin and the need for repentance, whereas Tertullian expected that believers had cast sin to the side.

a season of persecution. But Jesus gave no exception clause for forgiveness—freely we have been forgiven, and freely we should forgive.

After confessing guilt and seeking forgiveness, the Lord teaches that we pray, 'Lead us not into temptation, but deliver us from evil.' From these words Cyprian draws the conclusion that 'nothing is permitted to evil unless power is given from [God].'[27] Why would Jesus teach us to pray for God to keep evil away from His children unless He had the power to do it? Because God is for us, and because He is more powerful than the evil one, the Christian has nothing to fear. 'For what fear is there in this life,' Cyprian asks, 'to the man whose guardian in this life is God?'[28]

More than giving us words to pray, Jesus' life was an extended example of prayer. Jesus frequently prayed, seeking places of solitude, rising early to pray, and sometimes praying through the night. Cyprian employs the greater to lesser argument to demonstrate our need of prayer. 'But if He prayed who was without sin, how much more ought sinners to pray; and if He prayed continually, watching through the whole night in uninterrupted petitions, how much more ought we to watch nightly in constantly repeated prayer!'[29] These words fly like a flaming arrow into the heart of his reader. If ever there was someone who did not need prayer, then it was the perfect Son from heaven who was not entangled in sin. And yet, Jesus spent all of His days in prayer, seeking the Father continually. How much more, Cyprian asks, do we who stumble and fall into sin need to be at the throne of God for forgiveness of sin and protection from evil?

The manner in which prayers should be offered mattered too. In keeping with the importance of prayer as communal, the congregation would stand to pray and the priest would prepare the hearts of his people saying, 'Lift up your hearts,'

---

27 Cyprian, *On the Lord's Prayer* 25.

28 Cyprian, *On the Lord's Prayer* 27.

29 Cyprian, *On the Lord's Prayer* 29.

and the people would respond, 'We lift them up unto the Lord.' Those familiar with modern Catholic liturgy recognize this as the *sursum corda*, meaning 'lift up your hearts,' which is spoken just before the Eucharist is distributed, and dates back to at least the third century. This moment of preparation was to 'let the breast be closed against the adversary, and be open to God alone.'[30] Those in Cyprian's day were just as prone to wander in their thoughts when they prayed, which is why they vocally prepared their hearts for the seriousness of the moment. Cyprian cautioned against flippancy in prayers, saying, 'But what carelessness it is, to be distracted and carried away by foolish and profane thoughts when you are praying to the Lord, as if there were anything which you should rather be thinking of than that you are speaking to God! How can you ask to be heard of God, when you yourself do not hear yourself?'[31] In prayer we enter the very presence of God, which demands the full attention of our heart and mind.

For Cyprian, piety begins with prayer, or to say it conversely, there is no piety where prayer is absent. The theme of prayer saturates his writings, giving the impression that prayer is as important as breathing for the Christian. Pontius said these sweet words of Cyprian, 'Indeed, such was his love of sacred discourse, that he wished that his prayers in regard to his suffering might be so answered, that he would be put to death in the very act of speaking about God.'[32]

Virtue — the white crown

Prayer, or 'sacred discourse,' when prayed in the mold that Christ gave us, is 'spiritually abundant in virtue.'[33] Prayer and virtue are inseparable and they feed one another—virtuous people pray,

---

30 Cyprian, *On the Lord's Prayer* 31.

31 Cyprian, *On the Lord's Prayer* 31.

32 Pontius, *The Life and Passion of Cyprian* 14.

33 Cyprian, *On the Lord's Prayer* 9.

and prayer leads to greater virtue. Like prayer, the idea of virtue saturates Cyprian's writings, and this is why many Protestants have steered clear of the bishop of Carthage, wrongly thinking that virtue necessarily equates to works righteousness.

In far too many sectors of modern evangelicalism the aspect of grace in the gospel has been so overemphasized that any mention of virtue or good works is forced to the side and labeled legalism. The gospel, which we might define as the good news of Jesus Christ saving people from their sins through His life, death, and resurrection, all while creating a kingdom community of virtuous people committed to human flourishing, becomes lopsided when either faith or works are disproportionately emphasized.

A definition of virtue, as it appears in Cyprian, is well in order. Virtue is living in a way that pleases God, both in piety towards God and in love for others, as it is expressed through deeds. And more than just deeds, virtue is about being a certain type of person. Pontius praised Cyprian for the richness of his virtue, giving plenty of examples of how virtue worked itself out in Cyprian's life.[34]

> His virtue remained established in its own home, and his devotion, founded upon deep roots, gave way under no onset of the devil tempting him to abstain from blessing his God with a grateful faith even in his adversity. His house was open to every comer. No widow returned from him with an empty lap; no blind man was unguided by him as a companion; none faltering in step was unsupported by him for a staff; none stripped of help by the hand of the mighty was not protected by him as a defender. Such things ought they to do, he was accustomed to say, who desire to please God.[35]

---

[34] J. Patout Burns reminds us that in the *vita* Pontius 'may well have taken the opportunity to exaggerate Cyprian's virtue' (*Cyprian the Bishop* [Routledge Early Church Monographs; London and New York: Routledge, 2002], p. 207 n. 2) in an attempt to keep Cyprian's legacy alive after his martyrdom.

[35] Pontius, *The Life and Passion of Cyprian* 3.

The last sentence helps immensely in defining virtue in Cyprian's thought. Virtuous deeds are those things that are done by those who wish to please God. Virtue springs forth from personal devotion to God into action for others, as the ultimate fulfillment of Jesus' command of the double love (Matt 22:37-40).

Cyprian refused to accept that a person could be truly virtuous in word only. 'There is no advantage in setting forth virtue by our words, and destroying the truth by our deeds.'[36] He would not have recognized anyone who pontificated about virtue but who did not follow through in deed, or worse, denied the virtue of which they spoke with vice. Simply put, for Cyprian, one is not a Christian who does not live virtuously. Cyprian makes no apology for this. He does not try to think of the hypothetical person who believed rightly but did not act in accord with their belief. Obviously something is wrong with the thinking and belief if there is no outworking of action. A person cannot have true faith in Jesus Christ and not seek to fulfill the needs of others.

Several of Cyprian's writings deal practically with how the Christian can live a virtuous life. He wrote *On the Dress of Virgins* to instruct unmarried women on how to conduct themselves.[37] He opens the treatise saying, 'Discipline, the safeguard of hope, the bond of faith, the guide of the way of salvation, the stimulus and nourishment of good dispositions, *the teacher of virtue*, causes us to abide always in Christ, and to live continually for God, and to attain to the heavenly promises and to the divine rewards.'[38] Discipline, the 'teacher of virtue,' should not be viewed as a strict

---

36 Cyprian, *On Mortality* 20.

37 The dress of virgins must have been an important topic since Tertullian wrote a very similar treatise. Michel Fahey detects Stoicism underneath Cyprian's ethical constraints: 'Despite Cyprian's repudiation of Stoicism, Stoic influence may underlie his ethical strictures against cosmetics, hair-dyeing, the theatre, and property, and his disdain for the body' (*Cyprian and the Bible: a Study in Third-Century Exegesis* [Tübingen: J. C. B. Mohr, 1971], p. 28).

38 Cyprian, *On the Dress of Virgins* 1, emphasis added.

perimeter that confines the individual, but rather the arena in which faith and hope are free to flourish.[39] By living for God, in faith and virtue, she places herself on the path of salvation. The virgin glorifies God in her dress by turning aside lust and by avoiding the unchaste, immodest dress of harlots.[40]

Cyprian also wrote a short treatise on the virtue of patience, called *On the Advantage of Patience*. Patience was considered a virtue by many ancient philosophers, but Cyprian says that these philosophers 'pursue this virtue; but in their case the patience is as false as their wisdom also is.'[41] Philosophers may wax eloquent about the virtue of patience, but 'it is evident that patience is not real among them.'[42] Christians, on the other hand, 'do not speak great things, but live in them'; that is, they do not only talk about grand ideas like patience, they live patient lives. Patience may be a difficult virtue to cultivate, but 'whoever is gentle, and patient, and meek, is an imitator of God the Father . . . [and] what a glory is it to become like God!'[43] Jesus served as the supreme example of patience, since He endured scorn and shame as He bore the sins of humanity on Himself.[44] All of God's choicest servants,

---

39 G. W. Clarke remarks, '*Disciplina* is this man's favoured word (collapsing doctrinal teaching, church regulation and order, and moral duty)' ('Two Mid-Third Century Bishops: Cyprian of Carthage and Dionysius of Alexandria: Congruences and Divergences,' in *Ancient History in a Modern University*, ed. T. W. Hillard, et al. [Grand Rapids: Eerdmans, 1998], p. 321).

40 Cyprian, *On the Dress of Virgins* 6, 12.

41 Cyprian, *On the Advantage of Patience* 2. It is interesting that Cyprian attributes patience as a virtue to the philosophers. By Cyprian's day, the four cardinal virtues (temperance, prudence, courage, and justice), created by Plato and developed by Aristotle, were well established. It is difficult to know when patience was added to this list. The early church at some point added patience to the list, possibly because they conflated the fruit of the Spirit that Paul lists (Gal 5:22-23) with virtue. See Kossi Adiavu Ayedze, 'Tertullian, Cyprian and Augustine on patience: a comparative and critical study of three treatises on a stoic-Christian virtue in early North African Christianity' (PhD diss., Princeton University, 2000), for an analysis of patience in the thought of the three most important fathers of western North Africa.

42 Cyprian, *On the Advantage of Patience* 3.

43 Cyprian, *On the Advantage of Patience* 5.

44 Cyprian, *On the Advantage of Patience* 6. Notice that Cyprian here explains the atonement in terms of substitution.

from the patriarchs to the prophets, and all other righteous men who 'wore the figure of Christ,' 'were watchful over nothing more than that they should preserve patience.'[45]

For Cyprian, patience could be considered the pinnacle of virtue, which is interesting since patience gets so little attention in our day. He gives the reason why patience is foundational to virtue:

> It is patience which both commends and keeps us to God. It is patience, too, which assuages anger, which bridles the tongue, governs the mind, guards peace, rules discipline, breaks the force of lust, represses the violence of pride, extinguishes the fire of enmity, checks the power of the rich, soothes the want of the poor, protects a blessed integrity in virgins, a careful purity in widows, in those who are united and married a single affection. It makes men humble in prosperity, brave in adversity, gentle towards wrongs and contempts. It teaches us quickly to pardon those who wrong us; and if you yourself do wrong, to entreat long and earnestly. It resists temptations, suffers persecutions, perfects passions and martyrdoms. It is patience which firmly fortifies the foundations of our faith.[46]

Patience sounds as if it is the quintessential virtue for Cyprian, the virtue that demonstrates the culmination of all the other virtues. Cyprian likely wrote this work for two reasons: to exhort his fellow bishops to be patient in the midst of trials and to admonish his flock to wait patiently for the fulfillment of the Lord's promises.[47] Christians comprised such a small portion of the overall population in the mid-third century that it could have easily led to despair.[48] Not only were Christians few in

---

45   Cyprian, *On the Advantage of Patience* 10.

46   Cyprian, *On the Advantage of Patience* 20.

47   C. F. A. Borchardt, 'Cyprian on Patience,' *St Hist Eccl XVIII* 2 (1992): 19.

48   Estimates on the early Christian population are difficult to calculate. Rodney Stark, a sociologist and scholar of Christianity, has made a valiant effort at guessing the number down to the person. He estimates that there were 1,171,356 Christians in the Empire in A.D. 250, and hypothesizing that there were 60 million people in

number, but then they were targeted and their already small number dwindled because of martyrdom and apostasy. Hope was vanishing. From church leaders to new believers, Cyprian urged Christians to exercise patience as they waited on the Lord. Patience grows virtue.

The opposite of patience is jealousy and envy, the subject of another of his works, probably written when he noticed people were not adhering to his words on patience. If patience gives people contentment with what they already possess, then jealousy is the opposite, because it creates in people an insatiable desire for more. 'Jealousy,' warns Cyprian, 'has no limit; it is an evil continually enduring, and a sin without end.'[49] Jealousy is the antithesis of virtue because it replaces the love of God and neighbor with bitterness towards God, who did not give us what we wanted, and covetousness toward neighbors, who possess what we do not have.

The clearest presentation of Cyprian's thinking on virtue is found in his treatise *On Works and Alms*. A question that must be asked when talking about virtue is how (or where) does virtue play into salvation? Especially for evangelicals who have adopted the Reformation's doctrine of justification by faith, how ought we to think of virtue? More specifically for our purposes, does Cyprian place the right accent on virtue? The answer is complicated in part because Cyprian does not seem to have ever thought all the way through this issue, and so his comments can seem contradictory. The reason *On Works and Alms* is so important is because Cyprian seeks to demonstrate the importance of works, almsgiving in particular, and how they relate to salvation.

The opening of this book is critical. Cyprian states plainly that salvation begins with the work of God:

---

the Empire, that meant Christians made up 1.9 percent of the total population. See Rodney Stark, *The Rise of Christianity: How the Obscure, Marginal Jesus Movement Became the Dominant Religious Force in the Western World in a Few Centuries* (San Francisco: HarperCollins, 1997), p. 7.

49 Cyprian, *On Jealousy and Envy*, p. 7.

the large and abundant mercy of God the Father and Christ both has labored and is always laboring for our salvation: that the Father sent the Son to preserve us and give us life, in order that He might restore us; and that the Son was willing to be sent and to become the Son of man, that He might make us sons of God. . . was wounded that He might heal our wounds; served, that He might draw out to liberty those who were in bondage; underwent death, that He might set forth immortality to mortals. . . that more abundant care should be taken for preserving man *after* he is already redeemed![50]

God initiates salvation through His sending of His Son to die for the healing of mankind. *After* God saves, He gives a plan for those who have been redeemed, but the path laid out is for the purging of future sins. Cyprian ends his introductory paragraph by saying, 'Nor would the infirmity and weakness of human frailty have any resource, unless the divine mercy, coming once more in aid, should open some way of securing salvation by pointing out works of justice and mercy, *so that by almsgiving we may wash away whatever foulness we subsequently contract.*'[51] On the front side God saves by His mercy, but on the back side, God gives a way to wash away any sins committed after baptism, and the means provided is almsgiving.

Almsgiving as a means of cleansing post-baptismal sin was standard fare in the early church. In *2 Clement* the author exhorts, 'Charitable giving, therefore, is good, as is repentance from sin. Fasting is better than prayer, while charitable giving is better than both.'[52] John Chrysostom could preach in the fourth century, 'It is impossible, though we perform ten thousand other good deeds, to enter the portals of the kingdom without

---

50   Cyprian, *On Works and Alms* 1, emphasis added.

51   Cyprian, *On Works and Alms* 1, emphasis added.

52   *2 Clem.* 16.4, trans. Michael Holmes, *The Apostolic Fathers*, 3rd ed. (Grand Rapids: Baker Academic, 2007), p. 159. Holmes translates *eleēmosynē* as 'charitable giving' instead of as 'almsgiving.'

almsgiving.'[53] There was a steady witness in the fathers that almsgiving was a necessary part of Christian virtue.

In Cyprian's mind there was sufficient biblical warrant for this idea. He quotes the version of Proverbs 16:6 that was known to him: 'By almsgiving and faith sins are purged.'[54] Sins committed prior to initial faith are purged by the blood of Christ, but sins committed after conversion need to be expunged through works. Cyprian was not creative on this point—he was heir to a well-established tradition.[55]

Sin is like a wound that is healed by Christ's atonement, but these wounds reopen every time we sin, and so we must constantly patch them up with good deeds. This does not, however, invalidate the atonement. Christopher Hays keenly observes, 'advocates of redemptive almsgiving take pains not to displace the atonement of Christ.'[56] Cyprian in fact gives a vigorous defense of the sufficiency of the atonement and the need to repent: 'We have an advocate and an intercessor for our sins, Jesus Christ the Lord and our God, if only we repent of our sins past, and confess and acknowledge our sins, whereby we now offend the Lord, and for the time to come engage to

---

53   John Chrysostom, *Hom. Jo.* 23 as cited in Christopher M. Hays, 'By Almsgiving and Faith Sin are Purged? The Theological Underpinnings of Early Christian Care for the Poor,' in *Engaging Economics: New Testament Scenarios and Early Christian Reception*, ed. Bruce W. Longenecker and Kelly D. Liebengood (Grand Rapids: Eerdmans, 2009), p. 260.

54   In keeping with the scope of this book, the necessary textual work cannot be demonstrated fully. Briefly, the Masoretic text reads, 'By steadfast love (*hesed*) and faithfulness (*'emet*) iniquity is atoned for,' whereas the LXX text, as found in Proverbs 15:27a, reads, 'By almsgiving (*eleēmosynais*) and faith (*pistesin*) sins are cleansed (*apokathairontai*).' The idea of *hesed* evolved over time, from covenant faithfulness to the working out of covenant faithfulness in the care of others through alms. Cyprian quotes the book of Tobit, which also connects these ideas: 'Prayer is good, with fasting and alms; because alms does deliver from death, and it purges away sins' (Tobit 12:8-9). Cf. *2 Clem* 16.4; *Did* 4.5-6; *Barn.* 19.10.

55   On the tradition of redemptive alms in the early church before Cyprian, see Roman Garrison, *Redemptive Almsgiving in Early Christianity* (Sheffield: Sheffield Academic Press, 1993). Cyprian also quotes Sir 3.29-30: 'As water extinguishes fire, so almsgiving quenches sin.'

56   Hays, 'By Almsgiving and Faith Sin are Purged?' p. 267.

walk in His ways, and to fear His commandments.'[57] Christ died for sins to open up salvation; once one is saved, he continues in the path of salvation by obeying Christ's commandments, in particular through almsgiving. By mending our own wounds we actually propitiate God.

In one of the most troubling sentences in all of Cyprian's works, at least from a Protestant perspective, he states, 'The remedies for propitiating God are given in the words of God Himself; the divine instructions have taught what sinners ought to do, that by *works of righteousness God is satisfied*, that with the deserts of mercy sins are cleansed.'[58] The phrase 'works of righteousness' seems to stand in direct contradiction to Paul's claim that one is not justified on the basis of works (Gal 2:16; Rom 4:6; Tit 3:5; et al.), and that our sins are cleansed by faith in Christ's wrath-bearing substitution (Rom 3:21-26).[59] Cyprian probably understood Paul to teach that justification is by faith but that works are also necessary for maintaining salvation. A person is not justified by works or almsgiving, but he does assuage God's judgment on future sins by performing righteous acts. Thus, it is not getting in, but rather staying in that is the issue. Are we to write Cyprian off as one who abandoned central tenets of the gospel? Not quite.

Following in the footsteps of Paul, Cyprian appeals to Abraham as an exemplar of faith and works:

> For if Abraham believed in God, and it was counted unto him for righteousness, certainly he who gives alms according to God's precept believes in God, and he who has the truth of faith maintains the fear of God; moreover, he who maintains

---

57 Cyprian, *Letter* 7.5.

58 Cyprian, *On Works and Alms* 5, emphasis added.

59 The purpose here is not to get bogged down in what Paul meant. I am taking the traditional Lutheran approach that justification is a forensic declaration whereby one is forgiven of sins by faith apart from works.

the fear of God considers God in showing mercy to the poor. *For he labors thus because he believes.*[60]

This sentence is pregnant with Pauline themes that clarify the interplay between faith and works in his thought.[61] The appeal to Abraham and the careful ordering of the sentence cannot be underestimated. He follows Paul who points repeatedly to Abraham as the prototype for justification by faith (Rom 4; Gal 3). Abraham believed God and was justified (Gen 15:6), and his willingness to sacrifice his son was evidence of his faith (Gen 22). Belief in God preceded his work of righteousness. Likewise, the reason a person gives alms is because he has first believed in God; and because he fears God, he obeys God's command to give. Alms, then, are the physical demonstration of the inward belief.[62] A person labors *because* he believes.

In his letter on the Eucharist, he made a very similar point, again employing Abraham as an exemplar of faith: 'For if Abraham believed in God, and it was accounted unto him for righteousness,

---

60 Cyprian, *On Works and Alms*, 8.

61 Edwina Murphy is partially correct to say, 'Abraham is not employed to highlight the antithesis of faith and works but rather is shown to be the father of those who have faith, that is, those within the church' ('Divine Ordinances and Life-Giving Remedies: Galatians in the Writings of Cyprian of Carthage,' *Journal of Theological Interpretation* 8.1 [2014]: 99). The emphasis is on Abraham's example of faith. However, his juxtaposition of faith and works is highly significant in the flow of his argument. For justification in the century prior to Cyprian's, see Brian J. Arnold, *Justification in the Second Century* (Studies of the Bible and Its Reception 9; Berlin: Walter de Gruyter, 2017).

62 In *Letter* 13.1, Cyprian stated, 'Now he repents, who, remembering the divine precept, with meekness and patience, and obeying the priests of God, deserves well of the Lord by his obedience and his righteous works.' Phillip Campbell, in his editorial remarks on Cyprian's letters, comments, 'An excellent testimony to the fact that the early Church did not believe in justification by faith alone.' In my estimation, Campbell does not appreciate the broader context of Cyprian's view. John Faulkner noticed over a hundred years ago that Cyprian cannot be conceived of as a modern Catholic (or even a fourth-century Catholic). He writes, 'Ever and anon Christian sentiments burst forth, and principles both in doctrine and life thoroughly in accordance with the Gospel. For it is written, [Cyprian] says, that the just shall live by faith,' and that 'Cyprian looks upon justification in a thoroughly legal way' (see John Faulkner, *Cyprian: the Churchman* [Cincinnati: Jennings and Graham, 1906], p. 163).

assuredly whosoever believes in God and lives in faith is found righteous, and already is blessed in faithful Abraham and is set forth as justified.'[63] A person is justified on the basis of faith *and* living in faith, which almost certainly would have included things like the giving of alms, but the emphasis remains on the faith.

Cyprian motivated his people to almsgiving by reminding them of the final judgment. Christopher Hays writes, 'The church fathers most frequently dangled eternal salvation through alms in front of their recalcitrant or ungenerous audiences, like the proverbial carrot in front of a mule.'[64] Cyprian also nudged the rich to unclench their tight fists by assuring them that 'the wealth of the doer is increased by the retribution of God.'[65] Money has the power to hold one captive as a slave or the ability to free the soul from earthly concerns. Christians should seek the higher good—treasures in heaven (Matt 6:19-21).

Because his language is not always precise, it is easy to see how someone could misunderstand Cyprian to be teaching works righteousness as the grounds of salvation.[66] The course of salvation in his thinking, though never systematically fleshed out to my knowledge, appears to be this:

1. Salvation begins as a gracious act of God, flowing from His mercy.
2. God labored and continues to labor for our salvation, most significantly in the substitutionary death of Jesus.
3. We lay hold of salvation by faith.
4. We are saved in our baptism when we are cleansed from all our previous sins, either as adults (like Cyprian was) or as infants (like Cyprian argued).

---

63 Cyprian, *Letter* 62.4.
64 Hays, 'By Almsgiving and Faith Sin are Purged?' 271. cf. Cyprian, *Letter* 15.3.
65 Cyprian, *On Works and Alms* 9.
66 By the Middle Ages, almsgiving turned into the treasury of merit. But we cannot allow what became of almsgiving to be read back into Cyprian, just as a later view of penance cannot distort Cyprian's development of the doctrine.

5. To continue on the path of salvation, a person must be a part of the visible, catholic church and in subjection to the bishop.
6. Almsgiving and other virtuous acts purge us from further sins. A life of virtue is necessary to retain salvation.

Salvation was a holistic idea for Cyprian. He would have shunned the penchant for reductionism that plagues contemporary thought, which asks what the least common denominator is needed to see a person 'get saved.' Read this pamphlet, pray this prayer with all your heart, tell God you are sorry for your previous sins, walk an aisle, and then never give serious thought to the genuineness of your commitment, because this is from Satan and not God. This would have been nonsensical to Cyprian. An individual needs faith, the sacraments, the church, and perseverance. Salvation is an all-of-life commitment that must be demonstrated until life's final breath.

Faith and virtue are kept in tension, sometimes helpfully and sometimes less so, but even when he drifts towards works righteousness, he does not obscure the gospel. Roger Olson articulates well how we should think of faith and works in Cyprian:

> In spite of later Protestant polemics against the penitential system that grew out of Cyprian's theology, Cyprian himself was not guilty of works righteousness or self-salvation. Nowhere did he suggest that a person can earn salvation as a reward for good works; he only emphasized that a truly repentant sinner being saved by God's grace will necessarily demonstrate true repentance by outward acts.[67]

Overall, virtue serves to display and bolster faith in his thought. God commands Christians to live virtuously—anything short of virtue is a breach of faith. The reward for those who labor in charity is the crown Christ promised.

---

67 *The Story of Christian Theology: Twenty Centuries of Tradition and Reform* (Downer's Grove: InterVarsity Press, 1999), p. 120.

Cyprian takes one more chance to prod his reader to alms and good works as he closes *On Works and Alms*: 'the Lord will never fail of giving a reward for our merits: in peace He will give to us who conquer, a white crown for our labors; in persecution, He will accompany it with a purple one for our passion.'[68] Virtue is achieved by labor during peace and by martyrdom during persecution, as the color of our crown will testify.[69] Virtue culminates in suffering and death in Cyprian's theology, since martyrdom is the fitting end of the virtuous life.

Martyrdom — the purple crown

About 150 years before Cyprian was martyred, Ignatius of Antioch was taken to Rome in shackles as a condemned criminal, and then ushered into the Colosseum where he was mauled to death by lions. Ignatius described his forthcoming martyrdom with these gruesome words:

> May I have the pleasure of the wild beasts that have been prepared for me; and I pray that they prove to be prompt with me. I will even coax them to devour me quickly, not as they have done with some, whom they were too timid to touch. And if when I am willing and ready they are not, I will force them. Bear with me—I know what is best for me. Now at last I am beginning to be a disciple. May nothing visible or invisible envy me, so that I may reach Jesus Christ. Fire and cross and battles with wild beasts, mutilation, mangling, wrenching of bones, the hacking of limbs, the crushing of my whole body, cruel tortures

---

68 Cyprian, *On Works and Alms* 26. Cyprian's use of merit here just means that we will receive a reward for the works we do.

69 See Geoffrey D. Dunn, 'The White Crown of Works: Cyprian's Early Pastoral Ministry of Almsgiving in Carthage,' *Church History* 73.4 (2004): 715-40. Dunn argues that Cyprian was writing to encourage the confessors in prison that they would receive a reward even if they were not martyred. Cyprian extended this argument to the wealthy in Carthage in order to persuade them to almsgiving. Though they may not earn the purple crown of martyrdom, they could still receive the white crown of good works through their generosity.

of the devil—let these come upon me, only let me reach Jesus Christ![70]

Ignatius's desire for martyrdom, which comes across masochistic, hardly seems appropriate, and many scholars have questioned the soundness of his mind. Robert Louis Wilken said Ignatius had a 'vivid and flamboyant imagination,'[71] W. H. C. Frend claimed Ignatius's letters reveal 'a state of exaltation bordering mania,'[72] Allen Brent called Ignatius 'disturbed,'[73] and G. E. M. De Ste. Croix said he had a 'pathological yearning for death' that displayed his 'abnormal mentality.'[74] Far from being pathological, disturbed, or flamboyant, Ignatius knew that the lions were merely his vehicle to heaven. He wanted to attain God more than anything, and God had called him to martyrdom.

Ignatius may have been the first to write of martyrdom in such glorified language, but this became the trend in the early church.[75] Over the next century and a half martyrdom became the zenith of spirituality, so much so that the early church has often been referred to as the Church of Martyrs. In a time and place where many Christians are removed from the threat of martyrdom, the rhetoric of the fathers can sound disconnected from biblical spirituality. Why was Cyprian so emphatic in his treatment of martyrdom? Or, we might ask, how did martyrdom

---

70 See Ignatius, 'The Letter of Ignatius to the Romans,' 5.2–3, in *The Apostolic Fathers*, ed. and trans. Michael W. Holmes, 3rd ed. (Grand Rapids: Baker Academic, 2007), p. 231.

71 Robert Louis Wilken, *The First Thousand Years: A Global History of Christianity* (New Haven: Yale University Press, 2012), p. 29.

72 W. H. C. Frend, *Martyrdom and Persecution in the Early Church* (Oxford: Basil Blackwell, 1965), p. 197.

73 Allen Brent, *Ignatius of Antioch: A Martyr Bishop and the Origin of the Episcopacy* (New York: T&T Clark, 2007), p. 15.

74 G. E. M. De Ste. Croix, 'Why were the Early Christians Persecuted?' *Past and Present* 26 (1963): 23–24.

75 Cyprian could be just as grotesque in describing the devices of torture and death. 'The tortured stood more brave than the torturers; and the limbs, beaten and torn as they were, overcame the hooks that bent and tore them.' (Cyprian, *Letter* 8.1).

fit within Cyprian's spirituality? There are several answers that surface in his writings.

First of all, martyrdom was simply a reality for Christians in the first few centuries, and definitely so in the mid-250s. Because death and torture were always a possibility, Cyprian needed to make martyrdom appealing so that people would not drown in fear under the next wave of persecution. Persecution had revived in 257 under Emperor Valerian and once more everyone had to sacrifice to the Roman gods or face punishment. Cyprian refused to run and hide this go-round. That year he wrote a brief piece to Fortunatus entitled *Exhortation to Martyrdom* in which he sought to 'animate the soldiers of Christ for the heavenly and spiritual contest,'[76] which could be read side by side with his earlier work *On Mortality*, since both works prepared people for death.

Cyprian's words soared the highest when he wrote on suffering and martyrdom. Since much of his ministry was preparing people for their untimely deaths, either by sword or by sickness, it required a skillful tongue that could excite people to die. After all, those who had a communion with Christ, those who had been united to Him by faith, those who were strong in virtue, those who had been washed in the laver of regeneration, those who had become soberly intoxicated by His blood in the Eucharist, those who had participated in the church, and those who despised the world and longed for heaven, should not fear death but rather desire death to hasten. Death is freedom from a world that hates Christians into a world for which we were created, a world where Christ reigns and Satan exerts no influence. Fear of death makes no sense for the believer. When looked at from this angle, 'death is not feared but desired.'[77]

---

[76] Cyprian, *Exhortation to Martyrdom* 1. The Fortunatus to whom this is addressed is probably not the same Fortunatus we have met in previous pages.

[77] Cyprian, *Letter* 15.3.

Believers could embrace death as a pathway to paradise or cower in fear—either way, death was coming. Early authors needed a vocabulary that would incite courage for those who would be called on to die. Cyprian encouraged the faithful to see martyrdom as the highest spiritual calling, and thus to desire martyrdom without seeking it out. 'It is one thing,' says Cyprian, 'for the spirit to be wanting for martyrdom, and another for martyrdom to have been wanting for the spirit.'[78] He may have had Revelation 6:11 in mind that says God has preordained a precise number of martyrs. If God has marked one for martyrdom, he should consider himself blessed and submit gladly. There is nothing greater to which God could call a person.

Second, martyrdom acts like a whetstone that sharpens the double-edged blade of faith and virtue. Living under the ominous cloud of persecution should create in Christians a greater desire for virtue and faith. To the world this is foolish. In speaking more broadly about suffering, Cyprian writes, 'This, in short, is the difference between us and others who know not God, that in misfortune they complain and murmur, while adversity does not call us away from the truth of virtue and faith, but strengthens us by its suffering.'[79] Those without Christ have no category for suffering. To them, suffering is an interruption to the good life as they perceive it. For the Christian, however, suffering is the God-ordained means by which our faith and virtue grow. Drawing from Sirach 27:5, Cyprian said, 'The furnace tries the vessels of the potter, and the trial of tribulation for just men.' The same could be said of Peter who wrote, 'you have been grieved by various trials, so that the tested genuineness of your faith—more precious than gold that perishes though it is tested by fire—may be found to result in praise and glory and honor at the revelation of Jesus Christ' (1 Pet 1:6b–7), and of James who

---

78 Cyprian, *On Mortality* 17.

79 Cyprian, *On Mortality* 13.

made the audacious claim, 'Count it all joy, my brothers, when you meet trials of various kinds' (James 1:2). There was certainly no shortage of virtue-building trials in the mid-third century.

Suffering is not accidental and it should not be squandered, since God is working in and through the trials for the good of His children. Cyprian argued that courage in the face of death is 'profitable as a proof of faith.'[80] The goal of our suffering is to demonstrate the reality of our faith and to further build it up. We do not suffer for the sake of suffering. God is not bloodthirsty. Cyprian wrote, 'For God does not ask for our blood, but for our faith.'[81] God knows that he has the fullness of our faith when we would rather die than deny Him.

Interestingly enough, the reason a Christian should not fear death is because they have been justified by faith. 'Who. . . is trembling and sad, except he who is without hope and faith?' asks Cyprian. 'For it is written that the just lives by faith. If you are just, and live by faith, if you truly believe in Christ, why, since you are about to be with Christ, and are secure of the Lord's promise, do you not embrace the assurance that you are called to Christ, and rejoice that you are freed from the devil?'[82] The faith that saves is also the faith that helps us endure trials. And should not death, which brings us into Christ's presence and out of Satan's reach, be preferred to life anyway? If our faith reaches its completion at death, then martyrdom is a gift from God. Knowing that death lurks in the shadows of the future should produce a wealth of faith and virtue in the present.

Third, martyrdom is a second baptism. Cyprian argues, 'in the baptism of water is received the remission of sins, in the baptism of blood the crown of virtues.'[83] Leading up to this sentence, Cyprian wrote,

---

80 Cyprian, *On Mortality* 14.

81 Cyprian, *On Mortality* 17.

82 Cyprian, *On Mortality* 2–3.

83 Cyprian, *Exhortation to Martyrdom* preface 4.

> Let us only who, by the Lord's permission, have given the first baptism to believers, also prepare each one for the second; urging and teaching that this is a baptism greater in grace, more lofty in power, more precious in honor—a baptism wherein angels baptize—a baptism in which God and Christ exult—a baptism after which no one sins anymore—a baptism which completes the increase of our faith—a baptism which, as we withdraw from the world, immediately associates us with God.
>
> The baptism of blood is to be desired even more than the initial baptism of water. Those who had not yet undergone the baptism of water and Spirit should not fret, since the baptism of blood was strong enough to wash away sin, having more grace and more power. Baptism formed a great *inclusio* to his Christian life. Born the first time in water by the Spirit, and born again into everlasting life in the blood of his martyrdom. This is why early Christians celebrated the birthdays of the saints on the date of their death, since that is when they were released from this temporary life into the life that will have no end.[84]

Martyrdom was thus called the 'purple confession'[85] or the 'purple crown.'[86] The white crown was for virtuous works, but the purple crown belonged to those who died for their faith, which was the ultimate display of virtue. When Cyprian was converted to Christianity he removed his worldly purple garments. His purple robes embroidered with gold symbolized his old life that had to be laid aside in order to pursue Christ. However, he was able to take up purple garments again in his martyrdom.

Cyprian asked his reader to envision a voyage where the seas stir and begin to rage, tossing the boat violently against the waves.[87] Anyone in that situation would seek a harbor with haste.

---

84 Hence Cyprian's feast day celebrated on September 16, just two days after he had been killed.

85 Cyprian, *Letter* 20.1. This letter is from Celerinus to Lucian, yet it is still included in the corpus of Cyprian's letters. Speaking of martyrdom as the 'purple confession' was commonplace in the third century.

86 Cyprian, *On Works and Alms* 26.

87 Cyprian, *On Mortality* 25.

In this metaphor, the sea represents the present world with all of its trouble and uncertainties. The harbor is heaven that we can only reach through death. We should seek the heavenly harbor with its promise of peace and security in order to escape the treacherous seas of this world. Death, in Cyprian's thinking, is transformed into life. Unbelievers think that this world is safe and that death is to be feared; the Christian sees this world as unsafe and death to be embraced. In this world we are nothing but pilgrims and strangers on our way to our true country in paradise.[88]

Below the surface of Cyprian's rough exterior was a lively spirituality. He was not the 'cold disciplinarian' he is often portrayed as being. He loved God as his Father, Jesus as his Savior, the Holy Spirit as his guide, and the church as his mother. Coursing through his writings, even in the throes of polemical debate, was an unremitting piety built upon prayer, virtue, faith, and a willingness to die. He beckons all who would come after him to move forward in virtue:

> Let us confirm one another by mutual exhortations, and let us more and more go forward in the Lord; so that when of His mercy He shall have made that peace which He promises to give, we may return to the Church new and almost changed men, and may be received, whether by our brethren or by the heathen, in all things corrected and renewed for the better.[89]

---

88 Cyprian, *On Mortality* 26.

89 Cyprian, *Letter* 6.6.

5

CYPRIAN AND CONTEMPORARY CHRISTIANITY

The poet Prudentius (b. 348) eulogized Cyprian just over one hundred years after his death with these words: 'for though [Carthage] was Cyprian's home, indeed he was a glorious teacher of the world.... The power of his tongue is everywhere, which alone outlives his body, it alone knows not death.'[1] Cyprian's body may have been slain in 258, but the influence of his writings helped shape the church, outline the contours of orthodoxy, and give spiritual vitality to saints throughout all generations, giving him a sense of immortality. His tongue could not be silenced because his writings had already gone forth.

The goal of this series is to reintroduce evangelicals to our past for the purpose of help in the present. Cyprian remains a glorious teacher of the church today for those who will dust off the pages of history and read him. In this spirit I want to offer three areas where modern evangelicals would benefit by retrieving Cyprian: ecclesiology, virtue, and suffering and martyrdom.

First, Cyprian prized the church. His writings demonstrate the necessity and nature, as well as the polity and practices, of

---

[1] Prudentius, *Peristephanon liber, poema* 13, as cited by Ryan Grant, 'Introduction,' in *The Complete Works of Saint Cyprian of Carthage*, ed. Phillip Campbell (Merchantville, N.J.: Evolution Publishing, 2013), p. xv.

the church. Cyprian witnessed a desperate need to define the church in his day, and I see the same need in ours. To begin with, Cyprian reminds us that the church is necessary for our souls. Roger Olson summarized his legacy saying, 'Cyprian's significance in the story of theology lies. . . in his innovative linkage between ecclesiology and soteriology—between the doctrine of the church and the doctrine of salvation.'[2] In an age when the church is something to take or leave, Cyprian presses us to see the church as something essential to salvation. Where I pastored in western Kentucky, I frequently heard about a 'Christian' who had professed faith decades ago but had not darkened the door of a church since his baptism. No one dared challenge the legitimacy of his faith. No one told him that his soul was in jeopardy. To do such a thing would be to add to salvation by faith alone, or so it is thought. This problem is not unique to the so-called Bible belt. I have witnessed this exact same thing in Arizona and Ohio, and I suspect the same is true everywhere. We should consider reissuing Cyprian's clarion call for the centrality of the church, telling people that they should not consider God to be their Father unless they have a visible, local church as their mother. Again, we might want to stop just short of adding church membership to salvation as Cyprian would, but we should give people serious doubt about the state of their souls if they slough off the church.

Cyprian also helps us think about the nature of the church, both in regard to polity and our view of the sacraments/ordinances. I assume that the vast majority of people reading this book are not in an episcopal form of church polity, meaning there is no bishop overseeing their churches. What, then, can Cyprian teach us about church structure? Many things, but I will suggest just one. Cyprian instructs us that there is an authority structure in the church. Western democracy has infiltrated the

---

2   Roger Olson, *The Story of Christian Theology: Twenty Centuries of Tradition and Reform* (Downer's Grove: InterVarsity Press, 1999), p. 114.

church to the degree that everyone thinks they have equal right to dictate the course of the church, regardless of their spiritual maturity. Granted, there does seem to be biblical precedence for congregations as a final stamp of approval (Acts 15), but the teaching of the New Testament seems clear that leadership in the church is to be divided among a plurality of elders (Titus 1:5; 1 Tim. 5:17; et al.). We must encourage those in the church to submit to their leaders as to the Lord, since shepherds will have to give an account for the souls in their flock (Heb 13:17), just as we should encourage shepherds to lead their flocks with grace, remembering that they are simply under-shepherds (1 Pet 5:1-5). Cyprian demands respect for those whom Christ has called to lead the church. So should we.

When considering the sacraments, Cyprian's writings should cause us to pause and reflect on the purpose and practice of the holy signs Christ gave His church. Although I do not see baptismal regeneration in Scripture, I do think baptism is more significant than the oft-used wedding ring illustration. The pastor stands before his congregation, removes his wedding band and says, 'Even without this ring, I am still married. Likewise, with or without baptism, a person is saved.' This illustration leaves many in the pews wondering why we even baptize at all. For Cyprian, and a host of other writers in church history, baptism was the initial rite of the Christian faith that brought salvation.[3] Baptism should fit somewhere on the spectrum between necessary for regeneration and useless sign—closer, I think, to the former.

Evangelicals would also do well to retrieve more of Cyprian's view of the Lord's Supper. I have come to cherish the idea of the Supper as sober intoxication. More than just remembering a blood-stained cross and an empty tomb, the Supper should create in us a longing to die more to the world and live more for Christ, such that we are intoxicated by the things of God and

---

[3] Bobby Jamieson has recently fleshed out the importance of baptism within a credo-baptist framework (*Going Public: Why Baptism is Required for Church Membership* [Nashville: B&H Academic, 2015]).

sobered to the things of this world. Expressions of unity, piety, and holiness should surround the signs of the church as they have for ages. I rarely hear the ordinances spoken of in this way among evangelicals, to our detriment.

Second, Cyprian reminds us that virtue is indispensable for Christian living. As we saw in chapter 4, Cyprian held faith and virtue in tension, recognizing the necessity of both. Too often we pit faith against works as if works are the antithesis of faith, instead of faith's evidence. Rather than encouraging Christians to increase in virtue, believers are told to avoid the idea of virtue because it is thought to be synonymous with legalism, and then we wonder why so many Christians are living for the world, even though we have given them no biblical category for virtue within which they can flourish. Christians only know freedom in Christ when they walk according to His statutes. I found myself continually challenged by this idea in Cyprian's writings.

Finally, Cyprian gives a framework for suffering, martyrdom, and death. Death is not something Christians should fear. In fact, for those who look forward to an eternity in heaven away from the troubles of this life, death is all gain. Persecution in particular is God's purifying fire that refines faith and virtue, and it is a powerful tool for evangelism. Should persecution visit the West, which it most likely will at some point in the future, the church will come face to face with the same issue that plagued the North African church in the middle of the third century.

How will we treat those who deny the faith? As we have seen, Cyprian carved a passageway between the rigorists and the laxists, both of whom misunderstood the gospel. The laxists will need to realize that the gospel demands allegiance unto death, which means that denying Christ is a serious offense; the rigorists must remember that the gospel extends forgiveness to those who falter. Understanding how the church needs to respond to persecution is not academic. Right now our brothers and sisters in Africa, Asia, and the Middle East are suffering and dying for their faith. As we minister to them, we will need the wisdom of Cyprian, or at least familiarity with the debates from long ago, if we are to help their churches in the present.

One final word is in order for those who are still unconvinced that we need someone like Cyprian. It is important to note that I am not calling for an uncritical recovery of Cyprian. There are places where evangelicals will want to distance themselves from him. His belief in the saving power of baptism and his belief that sin after baptism must be atoned through almsgiving are certainly problematic. He misunderstood justification at times and he did not fully appreciate the all-sufficient nature of Christ's atonement. He overemphasized the bishop and underemphasized the congregation. But this makes Cyprian all the more important. There is a mutual spotlight shone from him to us and from us to him. If we need to agree with everything someone said, then we will not retrieve wisdom from anyone. Tertullian was a Montanist, Gregory the Great overemphasized his role as pope, Anselm prayed to Mary, Luther's remarks about the Jews could be viewed as anti-Semitic, Calvin condoned burning a man at the stake, some Puritans were slave owners, and in one hundred years the church will not be able to stomach something that is rampant in front of our blind eyes. Church history is nothing more than the Holy Spirit working through vessels of clay.

Cyprian is the mixture of situational wisdom and timeless truths. He entered into the challenges of his day with boldness and clarity. Yet since the contemporary culture continually looks like his, we need to release him of the parochial bonds of the third century so that he might instruct us. Maurice Wiles is right to say, 'History has cast him for a wider role, that of influencing at a very deep level the theological thinking of the western Church for the subsequent seventeen hundred years.'[4]

---

4 Maurice F. Wiles, 'The Theological Legacy of St. Cyprian,' *Journal of Ecclesiastical History* 14 (1963): p. 142.

Subsequent church Fathers, those in the Middle Ages, and some Reformers, thought fondly of Cyprian, and it is time we remember why.

FURTHER READING

The Complete Works of Saint Cyprian of Carthage, ed. Phillip Campbell. Merchantville, N.J.: Evolution Publishing, 2013.[1]

Burns, J. Patout. *Cyprian the Bishop. Routledge Early Church Monographs.* London and New York: Routledge, 2002.

Haykin, Michael. *Rediscovering the Church Fathers: Who They Were and How They Shaped the Church.* Wheaton: Crossway, 2011.

Hinchliff, Peter. *Cyprian of Carthage and the Unity of the Christian Church.* London: Geoffrey Chapman, 1974.

Litfin, Bryan. *Early Christian Martyr Stories: An Evangelical Introduction with New Translations.* Grand Rapids: Baker Academic, 2014.

Wilken, Robert Louis. *The First Thousand Years: A Global History of Christianity.* Yale: Yale University Press, 2013.

---

1. On reading Cyprian, I recommend this one volume work. Within the *Complete Works*, I would read these first: *To Donatus; On the Unity of the Church; Letters* 58 and 62.

More from the Early Church Fathers *series...*

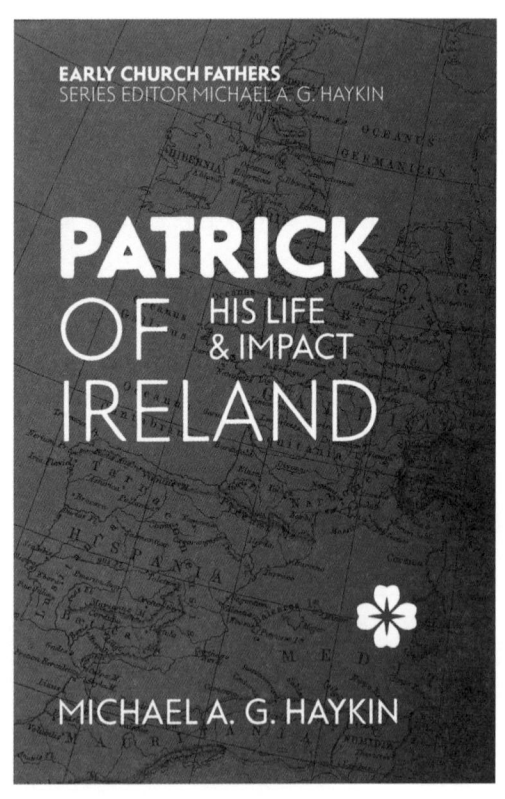

ISBN 978-1-5271-0100-5

PATRICK OF IRELAND

Michael A. G. Haykin

Patrick ministered to kings and slaves alike in the culture that had enslaved him. Patrick's faith and his commitment to the Word of God through hard times is a true example of the way that God calls us to grow and to bless those around us through our suffering. Michael Haykin's masterful biography of Patrick's life and faith will show you how you can follow God's call in your life. Early Church Fathers: this series relates the magnificent impact that these fathers of the early church made for our world today.

Michael A. G. Haykin is Professor of Church History and Biblical Spirituality at the Southern Baptist Theological Seminary, Louisville, Kentucky where he is also Director of the Andrew Fuller Center for Baptist Studies. He has written several books and is the series editor of the Early Church Fathers series.

Sometimes the historical figure outshines the legend. By sifting through reliable sources, Michael A. G. Haykin paints a compelling portrait of this bibliocentric bishop and earnest evangelist. The dedicated missionary and thoughtful theologian that emerges belongs to the Gospel-loving global church and not just the Emerald Isle. The persistent Patrick, a diligent minister of the Word and Spirit, deserves to be commemorated far more than once each year.

Paul Hartog
Adjunct Faculty – Biblical Studies,
Faith Baptist Bible College and Theological Seminary,
Ankeny, Iowa

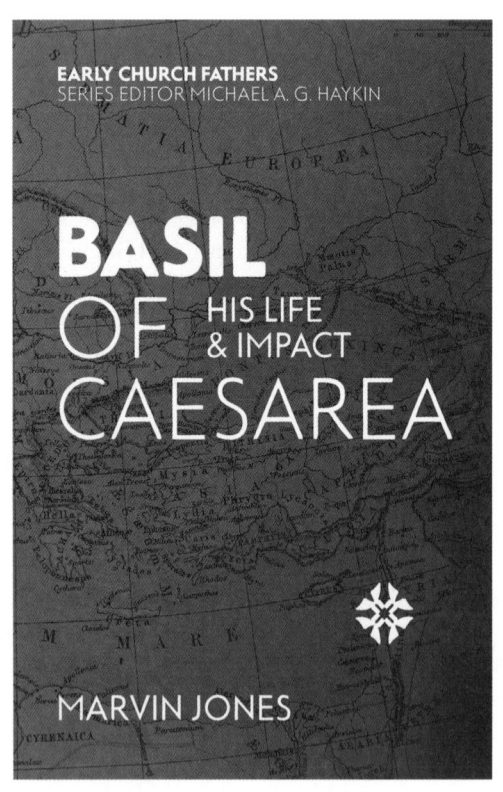

ISBN 978-1-78191-302-4

BASIL OF CAESAREA

Marvin Jones

Basil of Caesarea (A.D. 329–379) was a Greek Bishop in what is now Turkey. A thoughtful theologian, he was instrumental in the formation of the Nicene Creed. He fought a growing heresy, Arianism, that had found converts, including those in high positions of state. In the face of such a threat he showed courage, wisdom and complete confidence in God that we would do well to emulate today.

Marvin Jones is Chair of the Christian Studies Department and Assistant Professor of Church History and Theology at Louisiana College in Pineville, Louisiana. He holds degrees from Southeastern Baptist Theological Seminary, Dallas Theological Seminary and the University of South Africa.

There is a growing excitement about a series of volumes recounting the immense importance of the early Church Fathers in our circles and it is hugely encouraging to see this account of the significant life of Cyprian of Carthage by Brian Arnold. Immensely rewarding and full of exquisite detail, this book is a winner in every respect. More, please.

Derek W. H. Thomas
Senior Minister, First Presbyterian Church, Columbia, South Carolina,
Chancellor's Professor, Reformed Theological Seminary,
Teaching Fellow, Ligonier Ministries

Christian Focus Publications

Our mission statement –

STAYING FAITHFUL

In dependence upon God we seek to impact the world through literature faithful to His infallible Word, the Bible. Our aim is to ensure that the Lord Jesus Christ is presented as the only hope to obtain forgiveness of sin, live a useful life and look forward to heaven with Him.

Our Books are published in four imprints:

CHRISTIAN FOCUS

popular works including biographies, commentaries, basic doctrine and Christian living.

CHRISTIAN HERITAGE

books representing some of the best material from the rich heritage of the church.

MENTOR

books written at a level suitable for Bible College and seminary students, pastors, and other serious readers. The imprint includes commentaries, doctrinal studies, examination of current issues and church history.

CF4•K

children's books for quality Bible teaching and for all age groups: Sunday school curriculum, puzzle and activity books; personal and family devotional titles, biographies and inspirational stories – Because you are never too young to know Jesus!

Christian Focus Publications Ltd,
Geanies House, Fearn, Ross-shire,
IV20 1TW, Scotland, United Kingdom.
www.christianfocus.com